A Concise Junior Dictionary

Edited by **Iseabail Macleod**
and **Patrick McLaughlin**
with **Alasdair Anderson**

Schofield & Sims Ltd. Huddersfield

0 7217 0646 0
0 7217 0651 7 Net Edition

First Printed 1989
Reprinted 1990
Reprinted 1991
Reprinted 1992
Reprinted 1993

Designed by Graphic Art Concepts, Leeds
Printed by Butler & Tanner Ltd., Frome and London

Introduction

The aim of this book is to bridge the gap between very elementary picture dictionaries and more formal dictionaries compiled for older pupils. It is therefore intended mainly for children of seven to nine years, but it will of course also be useful outside that age group. Its chief purpose is to help children to learn to use reference material.

Definitions have been worded as simply as possible and involve an absolute minimum of technical jargon. In some cases this inevitably means a longer definition than would normally be necessary. Some definitions are worded in ways which omit certain concepts, see **familiar**, but every effort has been made to ensure that accuracy has been maintained.

Where more than one meaning of a word is included, the entry is divided accordingly, giving the most important meaning first; see **even**. Division into different parts of speech is not considered necessary at this level.

Pronunciation is very simply explained for a few words which might cause difficulty, e.g. **quay** (say 'key'). Where words with the same spelling are stressed differently, they are given separate entries, with the stressed syllable underlined, e.g. **record** and **record**.

In selecting the content, care has been taken to include words most useful to the child. It is inevitable however, that words will be omitted which, in the opinion of some, should have been included; for this the compilers can only say that it is impossible to include in a book of this scope *all* the words which even an average child might need. The class-room should provide a range of reference books for wider study.

In order to concentrate on the most useful material certain types of entry have been deliberately omitted. For instance pronouns, conjunctions and prepositions have been on the whole omitted on the grounds that they are unlikely to be looked up. If a word is used in more than one part of speech, normally only one is included for that meaning, e.g. **knock**. Likewise, derivative words such as **lightly**, **lightness** have also been left out, if their meaning is thought to be clear enough.

A separate booklet of exercises, *Concise Junior Dictionary Exercises* is available; it is based on the dictionary entries and gives further help in building up reference skills.

A a

abandon — *1* to leave, often for ever.
2 to give up.

abbey — a place where monks or nuns live.

abbreviation — a shortened word, for example **Dr** (Doctor), **Rd** (Road).

ability — being able to do things.

aboard — on(to) a ship or an aircraft.

abolish — to get rid of (something).

about — *1* concerning.
2 nearly.

above — *1* over.
2 higher than.

abreast — one beside the other, in line.

abroad — in or to another country.

abruptly — very quickly, suddenly.

absent — not here, not present.

absolutely — completely, quite.

absurd — silly, without any sense.

accent — the way people speak a language.

accept — to take something which is offered or given.

accident — something (bad) that happens by chance.

accommodation — somewhere to live or stay.

accompany — *1* to go with.
2 to play a musical instrument along with.

account — *1* a bill showing money to be paid.
2 a statement of money received and spent (for example from a bank).
3 a story.
account for to explain how something happened.

accurate — exactly right.

accuse — to say that someone has done something wrong.

ace — a high-scoring playing card.

ache — a pain in some part of the body.

achieve — to manage to do something, usually with effort.

acid — a strong liquid that can burn things.

acorn — the seed of the oak tree.

acquaintance — a person you know (slightly).

acrobat — someone who does leaping and balancing tricks (for example in a circus).

across — *1* from one side to the other.
2 on the other side of something.

act — *1* to do something.
2 a part of a play.
3 to perform on stage.

active — lively.

actor — a man who performs in a play, a film or on television.

actress	a woman who performs in a play, a film or on television.
actual	real; existing.
add	1 to put together with something else. 2 to find the total of two or more numbers.
adder	a small, poisonous snake found in Great Britain.
address	1 the house, street and town where you live. 2 to write to, to speak to.
adjective	a word which describes something.
admiral	the most important officer in the Navy.
admire	to think well of (someone or something).
admission	being allowed in (to a place or group); what you pay for this.
admit	1 to agree that something has happened or is true. 2 to allow (somebody or something) to enter.
adolescent	someone half way between being a child and an adult.
adopt	to take (someone else's child) into your family and care for it as if it were your own.
adore	to love very much.
adrift	floating on water helplessly in a boat or on a raft.
adult	a grown-up person.

advance	to move forward.
adventure	an exciting happening.
advertise	to make well-known (for example in a newspaper).
advice	what you say to someone to help them.
advise	to tell other people what you think they should do.
aerial	a wire which sends out or picks up radio or television signals.
aeroplane	a flying machine.
affect	to cause (things or people) to change.
affectionate	showing love for something or somebody.
afford	to be able to pay for.
afraid	frightened, full of fear.
after	behind; following.
afternoon	the time of the day between morning and evening.
afterwards	later.
again	once more.
against	1 on the opposite side (in a fight or a game). 2 next to and touching someone or something.
age	1 how old a person is. 2 a special time in history such as the **Stone Age.**
ago	in the past.
agony	very great pain.
agree	to think the same as.

aground	(of a boat) caught in sand or rocks in shallow water.
ahead	in front.
aid	help.
aim	1 to point at, for example with a gun. 2 to try to do something.
air	1 what you breathe. 2 to make (clothes or a room) fresh by letting air into them.
aircraft	an aeroplane.
airport	a place where aircraft land and take off.
ajar	partly open.
alarm	1 a warning bell or other sound. 2 a sudden fright.
album	1 a collection of things such as stamps in a book. 2 a long-playing record.
alert	ready to act, wide awake.
alike	the same, similar.
alive	living, not dead.
all	everything; everyone.
allergic	made ill by certain foods or things.
alley	a very narrow street between buildings.
alligator	a kind of crocodile.
allow	to let someone do something.
ally	someone who helps you (for example in a battle).

almond	a kind of nut (often used in cooking).
almost	nearly, not quite.
alone	by yourself.
along	from one end to the other.
aloud	in a voice loud enough to be heard.
alphabet	the letters of a language in a fixed order, A, B, C and so on.
already	1 by this time. 2 before this.
also	as well.
altar	the holy table in church.
alter	to make something different in some way, to change.
although	even if, though.
altogether	counting everybody or everything.
aluminium	a light, silvery-coloured metal.
always	for ever, at all times.
amazing	very surprising.
ambition	wanting very much to have or to do something.
ambitious	keen to do well at something.
ambulance	a van to carry sick or injured people.
amen	the ending of a prayer.
amid	in the middle of.
ammunition	things you can throw or shoot from a weapon to hurt others.

among	in the middle of, surrounded by.	**answer**	what you say or write when asked a question.
amount	a quantity, a sum (for example of money).	**ant**	a small insect that lives in large groups.
amuse	to make someone laugh or smile.	**antelope**	an animal like a deer, found in Africa.
ancestor	someone in your family who lived before you.	**anxious**	worried.
		any	one of many; some.
anchor	a heavy metal hook to stop a ship from moving.	**apart**	away from others; away from each other.
ancient	very old, belonging to long ago.	**ape**	a large monkey.
angel	someone who is believed to bring messages from God.	**apologize**	to say you are sorry for something you may have done or not done.
angle	the space between two straight lines which meet at a point.	**appeal**	to ask for something needed.
		appear	1 to come into view. 2 to seem to be.
angry	wanting to hurt or harm someone because of something.	**appetite**	the wish to eat.
animal	a living creature that can move.	**applaud**	to clap your hands together to show pleasure.
ankle	the joint between the leg and the foot.	**apple**	a round, hard fruit.
anniversary	the same date each year when something happened in the past.	**appoint**	to give a job to.
		appointment	a time set aside to see someone (for example a dentist).
announce	to say things to a lot of people.	**approach**	to come near to.
annoy	to make (somebody) upset or angry.	**apricot**	a round, soft, yellow fruit with a large, hard seed called a stone in it.
annual	1 happening every year. 2 a book which comes out each year.	**apron**	a piece of cloth you put on top of your clothes to keep them clean.
anorak	a waterproof jacket with a hood.	**aquarium**	a glass or plastic container in which fish are kept.
another	1 one more. 2 a different one.		

arch	a curved part of a building or bridge.	**artificial**	not natural, made by people.
architect	a person who makes the plans for a building.	**artist**	a person who makes pictures or sculpture.
area	1 a piece of land or sea. 2 the size of a surface.	**ash**	1 the grey powder left after a fire. 2 a kind of large tree.
argument	a disagreement, a fight with words.	**ashamed**	to feel bad about something you have done or not done.
arithmetic	working in numbers, adding, subtracting, multiplying and dividing.	**ashore**	on land.
arm	the part of the body between the shoulder and the hand.	**aside**	to one side.
		ask	1 to put a question to. 2 **ask for** to say that you want (something).
armour	a covering of metal worn by soldiers in battle.	**asleep**	sleeping.
army	a large number of soldiers.	**assembly**	a large group of people gathered together.
around	round the edges of, on all sides.	**assist**	to help.
arouse	to wake from sleep.	**astonish**	to surprise very much.
arrange	1 to put in the right order. 2 to make plans for.	**astray**	wandering away.
		astronaut	someone who flies in a spacecraft.
arrest	to make (someone) a prisoner.	**athletics**	sports such as running, jumping, etc.
arrive	to reach the place you are going to.	**atlas**	a book of maps.
arrow	1 the straight, sharp piece of wood which is shot from a bow. 2 a sign shaped like an arrow to show direction.	**atmosphere**	the air round the earth.
		attach	to fix on to something.
		attack	to start to fight.
		attempt	to try.
art	the making of pictures or sculpture.	**attend**	1 to be present. 2 **attend to** to look after.
article	1 a thing. 2 a piece of writing in a newspaper or magazine.	**attention**	care given to doing a job or in listening.

attic	a room just under the roof of a house.
attract	1 to win the liking of. 2 to make things come closer.
audience	people who listen to or watch a play or a concert, for example.
aunt	a father's or mother's sister; the wife of an uncle.
author	a person who writes books.
authority	the power to make people do what you want.
autograph	a person's name written by themselves.
automatic	working by itself.
autumn	the season between summer and winter.
available	able to be used, seen, etc.
avalanche	a large amount of snow suddenly rushing down a mountainside.
avenue	a road often with trees along the sides.
average	usual, ordinary.
avoid	to keep away from.
awake	not sleeping.
award	a prize for something you have done.
aware	knowing about something.
away	not here; not present.
awful	very bad.
awkward	1 clumsy. 2 difficult to use or deal with.

axe	a sharp-edged piece of metal on a long handle, used for chopping wood.
axle	the bar that joins the wheels of a car or cart.

B b

baby	a very young child.
bachelor	a man who is not married.
back	1 the part furthest from the front. 2 the part of the body between the neck and the bottom of the spine.
backbone	the long row of bones down the middle of your back, the spine.
bacon	salted or smoked meat from the back or sides of a pig.
bad	not good.
badge	a special sign you wear to show your school or club, for example.
badger	an animal with a black and white face which burrows in the ground.
badminton	a game like tennis played indoors.
bag	a container with an open top.
baggage	bags and cases used when travelling.
bail	1 a small piece of wood placed on the stumps at cricket. 2 to empty water from the bottom of a boat.

bait	something used in a trap or on a hook to attract an animal or a fish.
bake	to cook in an oven.
balance	1 to stay steady. 2 a machine for weighing things.
balcony	1 a raised floor in a theatre or cinema. 2 a platform outside a window.
bald	having no hair on the head.
bale	1 a large amount of goods or material tied together. 2 to empty water from the bottom of a boat.
ball	1 a round object, often used in games. 2 a special event with dancing.
ballet	a graceful dance, often one telling a story.
balloon	1 a toy of thin rubber which can be blown up. 2 a round bag which rises when filled with hot air or gas.
ballot	a kind of secret vote to choose someone.
bamboo	a kind of grass with stiff hollow stems.
ban	not to allow something.
banana	a long, sweet fruit with a yellow skin.
band	1 a group of musicians playing together. 2 a strip of material used to hold things together or as a decoration. 3 a group of people.

bandage	a strip of material used to wind round a cut or wound to protect it.
bandit	a thief, a robber.
bang	1 a sharp blow. 2 a sudden, loud noise.
bangle	a bracelet.
banish	to send away for a long time, especially out of a country as a punishment.
banister	a handrail beside a staircase.
banjo	a musical instrument played by plucking the strings.
bank	1 the side of a river. 2 a place where money is looked after. 3 a pile of earth or sand with sloping sides.
banner	a flag hanging from a pole, mast or rope.
banquet	a feast; a large public meal.
bar	1 a rod of metal or wood. 2 a division in music. 3 a counter where drinks and sometimes food are served.
bare	1 having no clothes or covering on, naked. 2 empty.
bargain	something bought cheaply.
barge	a boat with a flat bottom, used on a canal or river.
bark	1 the noise made by a dog. 2 the hard covering round a tree or branch.

barley	a kind of grain used as food and in making beer and whisky.
barn	a storehouse on a farm.
barrel	1 a large round container, flat at each end. 2 the long tube of a gun out of which the bullets are fired.
barrier	something put up to stop you going somewhere (for example a fence or a gate).
barrow	a small cart that is pushed.
base	1 the bottom part. 2 where someone or something started out from.
basement	a room or space under a building, a cellar.
basin	a round wide bowl, usually for washing in.
basket	a bag or container made of woven cane, straw, etc.
basketball	a game in which two teams try to throw a ball through a metal hoop.
bat	1 the piece of wood used to strike a ball (in cricket, for example). 2 a small, mouse-like animal that flies at night.
batch	a number of things together.
bath	a water container you can lie or sit in to wash yourself.
bathe	1 to swim or play in water. 2 to wash (a wound, for example).
battery	a closed container which stores electricity.
battle	a fight between two large groups of people.
bay	a place where the shore curves inwards.
bayonet	a long knife which is put at the end of a gun.
bazaar	1 a market in Eastern countries. 2 a sale of goods to raise money (for a church or a school, for example).
beach	land by the sea, usually covered with sand or small stones.
beads	small pieces of glass, wood, plastic, etc. which are threaded onto a string.
beak	the hard, pointed mouth of a bird.
beam	1 a large, heavy piece of wood or metal. 2 a ray of light.
bean	a seed of the bean-plant, used for food.
bear	1 a large, hairy animal with very strong teeth and claws. 2 to carry. 3 to put up with.
beard	hair growing on a man's face.
beast	an animal.

beat	1 to hit again and again. 2 to keep time in music with a stick. 3 to do better than (someone) in a game or fight.
beautiful	having very good looks, looking lovely.
beaver	a furry animal with a wide, flat tail which lives in or near water in cool lands.
bed	1 a piece of furniture for sleeping on. 2 a part of a garden where plants are grown. 3 the bottom of the sea or of a river.
bee	an insect with a sting which collects honey from flowers.
beech	a kind of tree with smooth, grey bark.
beef	meat from cattle.
beer	a strong drink made from barley.
beetle	an insect with wings which fold to form a hard back when it is not flying.
beetroot	a dark-red vegetable used in salads.
before	1 in front of; earlier than. 2 in past times.
beg	to ask someone for money or goods.
beggar	someone who lives by begging.
begin	to start.

behave	to act in a certain way, especially to act well towards others.
behaviour	the way you behave.
behind	at the back of.
being	something that is alive.
belief	what you feel to be true.
believe	to feel sure that something is true, to trust in something.
bell	1 a piece of rounded metal which rings when you hit it. 2 something which is rung to attract attention (for example a **doorbell**).
belong	1 to be your own. 2 to be a part of.
below	underneath; lower down.
belt	a narrow piece of cloth, leather, plastic, etc. worn round the waist.
bench	1 a long, wooden seat. 2 a work-table.
bend	1 a turn, a curve (for example in a road). 2 to make something turned or curved.
benefit	to do good to.
beret (say 'beray')	a soft round cap, sometimes worn by soldiers.
berry	a small, juicy fruit.
beside	at the side of, next to.
besides	also, too.
betray	to give away someone's secret.

better
1 finer than, nicer than.
2 less ill than you were.

between
1 in the middle of (two things or people).
2 shared by two people.

beware
to be very careful of.

beyond
farther on than.

Bible
the religious book of the Christians.

bicycle
a two-wheeled machine you sit on to ride.

bill
1 a piece of paper that shows the money you owe for something.
2 a bird's beak.

billiards
a ball game played on a table.

bin
a large box, especially one for putting rubbish in.

bind
to wrap round with rope or string, for example.

binoculars
a special pair of glasses to let you see far into the distance.

biology
the study of living things.

birch
a tree with a silvery-coloured bark.

bird
a feathered animal which has wings and can fly.

birthday
the day of the year when a person was born.

biscuit
a dry, thin cake.

bishop
the priest in charge of a large district such as a city.

bit
1 a small piece.
2 a piece of metal in a horse's bridle held in the mouth.

bite
to cut something with the teeth.

bitter
tasting sour, not sweet.

black
the darkest colour, the opposite of white.

blackberry
a wild, juicy fruit used as food.

blackbird
a kind of songbird. The male has black feathers.

blackboard
a board used for writing on with chalk.

blacksmith
someone who makes things out of iron (for example horseshoes).

blade
the part of a knife or sword used for cutting.

blame
to find fault with, to say who has done wrong.

blank
empty, with nothing written on it.

blanket
a warm bed-covering, usually made of wool.

blast
1 a sudden rush of wind.
2 to break something up by explosions.

blaze
to burn with bright flames.

blazer
a jacket, often with a badge on its top pocket.

bleach
to make something lighter or whiter in colour.

bleak
cold and dismal.

bleat
the sound made by sheep and lambs.

bleed	to lose blood.
blend	to mix together.
bless	1 to ask God to help somebody. 2 to wish happiness to.
blessing	1 something you are glad about. 2 asking or receiving God's help.
blind	1 not able to see. 2 a covering for a window.
blindfold	a covering for the eyes to stop someone seeing.
blink	to open and close the eyes quickly.
blister	a sore swelling on the skin with liquid inside it.
blizzard	a strong wind with heavy snow.
block	1 a thick piece of something (for example wood or stone). 2 to be in the way of. 3 a large building with a lot of flats or offices.
blond(e)	fair in colour.
blood	the red liquid which moves round your body.
blossom	the flowers of plants and trees.
blot	a dirty mark, especially an ink stain.
blouse	a light garment worn by women and girls on the top part of the body.

blow	1 to shoot air out of the mouth. 2 (of air) to move quickly. 3 a hit made with the hand or a weapon.
blue	the colour of the sky without clouds.
bluebell	a wild spring flower with small, blue, bell-shaped flowers.
blunder	a stupid mistake.
blunt	not able to cut, not sharp.
blush	when your face goes red because you are ashamed, excited or shy.
board	1 a flat piece of wood. 2 to go on to (a ship, a train or an aeroplane, for example).
boast	to speak too proudly about yourself or something that belongs to you.
boat	a small ship.
body	1 the whole of a person or animal which can be seen. 2 the body without the head, arms, legs (and tail).
bodyguard	a person or group whose job it is to keep someone safe from attack.
bog	wet earth, a swamp.
boil	1 a painful swelling on the body. 2 to heat water until it turns to steam. 3 to cook in hot water.

bold	brave, not afraid.
bolt	1 a fastener on a door. 2 a metal screw. 3 to rush away.
bomb	a shell which explodes.
bone	one of the hard parts of the body which make up the skeleton.
bonfire	a large fire built in the open air.
bonnet	1 the cover of a motor car engine. 2 a kind of hat.
book	1 a number of pages bound together. 2 to arrange for a seat (at the cinema, for example) to be kept for you.
boom	a loud hollow noise.
boomerang	a curved weapon, used by the natives of Australia, which can be made to return to the thrower.
boot	1 footwear which comes above the ankles. 2 a covered place for luggage in a car.
border	1 the edge of something. 2 the line where two countries meet.
bore	1 to make a hole. 2 to make (someone) fed up by talking in a dull way.
born	when something or somebody becomes alive.
borrow	to use something belonging to someone else with their permission.

bother	1 trouble. 2 to annoy.
bottle	a glass or plastic container for liquids, usually with a narrow neck.
bottom	1 the underneath part of something. 2 the part of your body you sit on.
boulder	a large stone or rock.
bounce	to (make something) spring up and down.
bound	1 to spring upwards and forwards. 2 tied together. 3 **bound to** very likely to.
boundary	1 the outside edge (for example of a cricket field). 2 the line where one piece of land touches another.
bouquet	a special bunch of flowers.
bow (rhymes with 'low')	1 ribbon with loops on it. 2 a weapon used to fire arrows. 3 the stick used when playing a violin.
bow (rhymes with 'now')	1 the front part of a boat. 2 to bend forward from the waist to show respect.
bowl	1 a deep, round dish. 2 to send the ball to the person batting (at cricket, for example). 3 the ball used in the game of bowls.

bowls	a game in which a large heavy ball is rolled along the grass.
box	1 a container, usually with a lid, often made of wood, cardboard or metal.
	2 to fight with the fists.
boy	a young, male child.
bracelet	a decoration worn on the wrist or arm.
bracket	a support for a shelf etc.
brackets	curved lines like this ( ) you sometimes put round words or figures.
brag	to boast a lot.
brain	the part of the head used for thinking etc.
brake	the part on a vehicle which makes it go slower or stop.
bramble	a prickly bush on which blackberries grow.
branch	the part of the tree on which the leaves grow.
brand	the name of a particular kind of goods made by one company.
brass	a yellowish metal made by mixing copper and zinc.
brave	not afraid, ready to face up to danger or pain.
bread	food made from flour, yeast and water baked together.

break	1 to cause something to fall to pieces.
	2 a short rest from what you are doing.
breakfast	the first meal of the day.
breast	the front, upper part of the body.
breath	air taken in and let out of your mouth and lungs.
breathe	to take air in and let it out of your lungs.
breed	1 the family or kind of an animal.
	2 to have and bring up young ones.
breeze	a gentle wind.
bribe	to give (someone) money so that they will help you dishonestly.
brick	a baked clay block used for building.
bride	a woman on her wedding day.
bridegroom	a man on his wedding day.
bridesmaid	a girl or young woman who attends a bride at her wedding.
bridge	1 something built to let you cross over a river, a road, or a railway.
	2 where the captain stands on a ship.
	3 a card game.
bridle	leather bands put on a horse's head to control it.
brief	short.
briefs	short underpants.

bright
1 shining.
2 clever.

brilliant
1 very bright, shining.
2 very clever.

brim
1 the top edge of a container such as a basin.
2 the part of a hat which sticks out at the edge.

bring
to take with you.

brisk
quick, lively.

bristles
short, stiff hairs like those on a brush.

brittle
hard yet easily broken.

broad
very wide.

broadcast
a radio or television programme.

broken
in pieces.

bronze
a metal made by mixing copper and tin.

brooch
(say 'broach')
an ornament which can be pinned to your clothing.

brood
1 a number of young birds hatched together.
2 to think deeply and to worry when there is no need to do so.

brook
a small stream.

broom
a stiff brush with a long handle.

brother
a boy or man who has the same parents as someone else.

brow
1 the forehead.
2 the top of a hill.

brown
the colour of earth or of chocolate.

bruise
a mark on the skin where it has been hit.

brush
1 a tool used for sweeping, scrubbing and painting.
2 a fox's tail.

Brussels sprouts
a vegetable like very small cabbages growing on a long stalk.

bubble
1 a hollow ball of liquid filled with air or gas.
2 to give off bubbles like water when it boils.

buck
a male deer or rabbit.

bucket
a container with a handle, often used for carrying liquids, a pail.

buckle
a fastener for a belt or shoe, for example.

bud
a leaf or flower before it opens.

budgerigar
a small, brightly-coloured bird often kept as a pet.

bugle
a musical wind instrument like a small trumpet.

build
to put up; to make into something.

building
a usually large structure with walls and a roof.

bulb
1 a flower root shaped like an onion.
2 the part of an electric light that shines.

bulge
to swell outwards.

bull
a male animal of cattle, elephant, whale, etc.

bulldozer
a large machine for moving earth to make it flat.

bullet	a piece of metal shot from a gun.
bully	someone who ill-treats those weaker than himself.
bump	1 a sudden knock. 2 a swelling on the body where it is hit.
bumper	a metal rail at the front and back of a vehicle.
bun	a small, round cake.
bunch	several things tied together.
bundle	many things tied or held together.
bungalow	a house by itself with all its rooms on one floor.
bunk	a bed sometimes fixed to a wall like a shelf, often with another above (for example on a ship).
buoy (say 'boy')	a fixed floating object which is placed somewhere to warn ships of danger.
burden	something heavy that is carried, a load.
burglar	a person who enters houses and shops to steal.
burial	the burying of a dead body.
burn	1 to be or to set on fire. 2 a sore place on the skin caused by heat.
burrow	an underground tunnel dug by an animal such as a rabbit.

burst	1 to blow into pieces. 2 to break open.
bury	to put (something) in a hole in the ground and cover it over.
bus	a large motor vehicle which carries passengers.
bush	a small tree.
business	work, trade.
busy	having no time to spare, doing a lot of things.
butcher	someone who sells meat.
butter	a fatty food made from cream.
buttercup	a bright-yellow wild flower.
butterfly	an insect with large, usually brightly-coloured wings.
button	a fastening for clothing which fits into a hole.
buy	to get something by giving money.
buzz	a low sound such as that made by some insects when flying.

C c

cab	1 a place for the driver of a lorry or train. 2 a taxi.
cabbage	a large, usually green, broad-leaved vegetable.
cabin	1 a room on a boat or an aeroplane. 2 a small, wooden house.

cable
1 wires that carry electricity or telephone calls.
2 a strong rope often made of wires twisted together.

cackle
to make a noise like a hen after it lays an egg.

cactus
a prickly desert plant with thick stems.

cadet
a young person being trained in the police, army, etc.

café
a place for eating, usually simple meals or snacks.

cage
a box or room made of wires or bars in which animals or birds are kept.

cake
a sweet, baked food made of flour, eggs, sugar, etc.

calculator
a small machine used to count very large or complicated numbers.

calendar
a sheet or book showing the days and months of the year.

calf
1 a young animal, usually a young cow or bull.
2 the soft back part of the leg between the knee and the ankle.

call
1 to shout to.
2 to visit.
3 to give a name to.

calm
quiet and still, peaceful.

camel
a humped animal used for carrying people and goods in the desert.

camera
a device for taking photographs.

camouflage
a form of dress or covering which makes people or things seem to be part of the background.

camp
1 a group of tents together.
2 to live in a tent.

can
a small sealed container made of tin.

canal
a man-made waterway.

canary
a yellow songbird sometimes kept as a pet.

candle
a stick of wax with a wick which is burned to give light.

cane
the hollow stalk of some plants, which can be made into a stick.

cannibal
someone who eats human flesh.

cannon
a heavy gun which fires shells.

canoe
a light boat moved by using a paddle.

canteen
a place where people eat together (in a factory or school, for example).

canvas
strong cloth used to make tents, sails, etc.

cap
1 a kind of head covering.
2 a lid or cover.

capable
able to do.

cape
a cloak to cover a person's shoulders and arms.

capital
1 the chief city or town.
2 a large letter such as A, B, Y or Z.

captain
1 the person who controls an aeroplane or a ship.
2 an officer in the army.
3 the leader of a team or group.

captive   a prisoner.

capture   to take prisoner, to catch.

car   a motor vehicle to carry people.

caramel   a chewy sweet.

caravan   a house on wheels.

card
1 a piece of stiff, thick paper.
2 a piece of card with a message and often a picture (for example sent on someone's birthday).
3 one of a set of cards used for playing games.

cardboard   very stiff, thick paper.

cardigan   a short woollen jacket.

care
1 to be concerned about.
2 the act of looking after someone or something.

caretaker   a person who looks after a building such as a school.

cargo   goods carried on a ship or aeroplane.

carnation   a sweet-smelling garden flower (usually pink, white or red).

carnival   a large procession, usually in fancy dress.

carol   a Christmas hymn.

carpenter   someone who makes things out of wood.

carpet   a thick, soft covering for a floor.

carriage
1 a part of a train where people sit.
2 a vehicle pulled by horses.

carrot   a long, orange root vegetable.

carry   to take from one place to another.

cart   a vehicle for carrying goods, often pulled by a horse.

carton   a box made of cardboard.

cartoon
1 a drawing in a book or newspaper, usually to make you laugh.
2 a short film made out of drawings.

carve
1 to shape wood or stone with cutting tools.
2 to cut meat into slices.

case
1 a kind of box to keep or carry things in.
2 a suitcase.

cash   money in notes and coins.

cask   a small barrel used to store liquids.

cassette   recording tape in a holder.

cast
1 people taking part in a play or film.
2 to throw.
3 something shaped in a mould.
4 the actors in a play.

castle	a large stone building with towers and strong walls.
catalogue	a list of things in a special order.
catch	1 to take hold of. 2 to get (an illness).
caterpillar	a worm-like creature with legs which will turn into a moth or butterfly.
cathedral	a very important church.
catkin	a kind of fluffy flower which grows on some trees, for example the willow.
cauliflower	a vegetable with a hard, white flower.
cause	to make something happen.
cautious	taking great care.
cave	a hollow place in rocks or in the earth.
cease	to stop doing something.
ceiling	the inside of the roof of a room.
celebrate	to remember something in a special way, especially by having a party or feast.
celery	a vegetable with long, whitish-green stalks.
cell	a room in which prisoners are kept.
cellar	a store-room under a building.
cello	a musical instrument like a large violin.

Celsius	a temperature scale of 100 degrees, formerly called **centigrade.**
cement	a stone dust which sets hard when mixed with water.
cemetery	a place where people are buried.
centigrade	a temperature scale of 100 degrees, now called **Celsius.**
centimetre	a measure of length equal to a hundredth part of a metre.
centipede	a crawling insect with a large number of legs.
central	1 in the middle. 2 important.
central heating	a way of warming a building by sending heat from a central point (for example through pipes).
centre	1 the middle of something. 2 a place where people come together to do things.
century	1 a hundred years. 2 a hundred runs at cricket.
cereal	1 a crop such as wheat, rice or oats used for food. 2 a kind of food made from grain and usually eaten for breakfast.
ceremony	a special service held to celebrate something.
certain	1 sure. 2 some, but not all.

certificate	a piece of paper which says something important about a person, for example.
chaffinch	a kind of small bird.
chain	a number of rings joined together.
chair	a piece of furniture for one person to sit on.
chalk	1 a soft, white rock which crumbles. 2 a white or coloured stick used for writing on a blackboard.
challenge	1 to offer to fight someone. 2 a test of ability.
champion	the winner over all the others in a competition.
chance	1 an unexpected happening. 2 a time when you can do something you want to do.
change	1 to become different. 2 money you get back when you pay more than is needed.
channel	a narrow strip of water.
chapter	a part of a story or book.
character	1 what someone is like as a person. 2 a person in a play or story.
charge	1 to rush at. 2 the price asked for something. 3 **in charge** in control of something.

chariot	(long ago) a horse-drawn cart used in battle.
charity	giving money to people who need it.
charm	1 a magic spell. 2 a small ornament which is supposed to bring good luck.
charming	pleasing to other people.
chart	1 a map used by sailors. 2 a piece of paper with information, often a drawing or a sketch.
chase	to run after.
chat	to talk in a friendly way.
chatter	to speak quickly, especially about things that don't matter.
chauffeur	a person whose job it is to drive a motor car for someone.
cheap	low in price, not costing a lot.
cheat	to act unfairly, to make others believe what is not true.
check	1 to make sure that everything is in order. 2 a pattern of squares.
cheek	1 one of the sides of the face between the nose and the ears. 2 rudeness.
cheer	to shout loudly for joy.
cheerful	full of fun, looking happy.
cheese	a solid food made from milk.

chemist	someone who sells medicines.	**chip**	*1* a tiny piece broken from something larger. *2* a thin piece of potato fried in deep fat.
cherry	a small, red fruit with a large, hard seed called a stone in it.	**chirp**	a noise made by young birds and some insects (for example grasshoppers).
chess	a game played by two people on a squared board.	**chisel**	a sharp steel tool used for cutting wood, stone or metal.
chest	*1* a large, strong box. *2* the upper front part of the body.	**chocolate**	a sweet food made from cocoa.
chestnut	the hard, brown seed of the chestnut-tree.	**choice**	the act of choosing; something you choose.
chew	to keep biting food in your mouth.	**choir**	a group of people singing together.
chicken	a (young) bird kept for its eggs and meat.	**choke**	*1* to be unable to breathe because of something in the throat. *2* to block up.
chief	*1* the person in charge. *2* the most important.	**choose**	to pick out what is wanted from a large number.
chilblains	painful itching on hands and feet caused by cold.		
child	a young boy or girl.	**chop**	*1* to cut up with heavy blows (for example with an axe). *2* a slice of meat with a bone in it.
chill	*1* coldness. *2* a slight cold which causes shivering.		
chilly	(of weather) quite cold.	**chopsticks**	two small sticks used by the Chinese and Japanese for eating with.
chime	the noise made by bells.	**chorus**	*1* part of a song or poem which is repeated after each verse. *2* a group of people singing together.
chimney	a pipe to take smoke away.		
chimpanzee	a kind of monkey without a tail.		
chin	the part of the face below the bottom lip.	**christening**	when a baby is given its name in a Christian church.
china	fine pottery, especially cups and saucers and plates.	**Christian**	a believer in Jesus Christ.

chuckle	to laugh quietly.	**clasp**	1 to grip or hold tightly.
chum	a close friend.		2 a fastening.
chunk	a thick piece cut off from something larger.	**class**	1 people who are taught together.
church	a building in which God is worshipped.		2 a group of people or things of the same kind.
cider	a strong drink made from apples.	**clatter**	a loud rattling noise.
cigar	dried tobacco leaves rolled tightly together and used for smoking.	**claw**	the sharp, hard nails of a bird or an animal.
cigarette	cut-up tobacco leaves rolled in a paper tube for smoking.	**clay**	sticky earth from which bricks and pottery may be made.
cinder	a piece of coal which has been partly burned.	**clean**	not dirty or dusty.
cinema	a place where films are shown.	**clear**	1 easy to see, hear or understand.
circle	something round, a ring.		2 to put away, to tidy.
circumference	the outside edge of a circle.	**clerk** (say 'clark')	a person who attends to letters etc. in an office.
circus	a travelling show of acrobats, clowns and (sometimes) animals.	**clever**	1 quick at learning and understanding things.
city	a large town (in Britain, one with a cathedral).		2 skilful.
claim	to say that something belongs to you.	**click**	a small, sharp noise.
clang	the sound made by a large bell.	**cliff**	high, steep land often overlooking the sea.
clap	1 to slap the hands together quickly.	**climate**	the sort of weather a place usually has.
	2 the sound made by thunder.	**climb**	to go up a steep place.
clarinet	a musical instrument played by blowing.	**cling**	to hold on tightly.
clash	to bump together noisily.	**clinic**	a place where doctors and nurses give help to people.
		clip	1 a fastener.
			2 to cut with a pair of shears or scissors.
		cloak	a loose covering without sleeves for the body and arms.

clock	a machine for telling the time.	**coach**	1 a passenger vehicle such as a bus or a railway carriage.
clockwork	machinery which is worked by winding a spring.		2 a person who gives special training (for example to a football team).
close (rhymes with 'dose')	near.	**coal**	a black rock dug out of the ground burned to make heat.
close (rhymes with 'doze')	to shut.	**coarse**	rough, not fine.
cloth	1 material for making clothes or curtains, for example.	**coast**	the strip of land next to the sea.
	2 a piece of cloth for cleaning something.	**coat**	1 an outer garment with sleeves.
			2 the hair of an animal.
cloud	a mass of rainy mist floating in the sky.	**cobweb**	a net made by a spider to trap insects.
clover	a small flowering plant with leaves in three parts.	**cock**	a male bird.
		cocoa	a brown powder from which chocolate is made.
clown	a person who acts foolishly to make people laugh.	**coconut**	the very hard, hairy fruit of a kind of palm tree, filled with milky juice.
club	1 a heavy stick.	**cod**	a large sea-fish used as food.
	2 a group of people who meet together for a special purpose.	**code**	1 writing with a hidden meaning.
	3 a stick used to play golf.		2 a set of rules (for example the **Highway Code**).
	4 one of the four kinds in a pack of playing cards.		
clue	something which helps you to find the answer to a puzzle or a question.	**coffee**	a drink made from the roasted and crushed seeds of the coffee tree.
clumsy	awkward in the way you move or do things.	**coffin**	a box in which a dead body is put.
cluster	a bunch or a group of things.	**coil**	to gather rope, wire or piping in rings (one on top of the other).

coin a piece of metal used as money.

coke 1 baked coal from which gas has been taken.
2 **Coke** a refreshing, fizzy drink.

cold 1 not hot.
2 an illness which makes your nose run.

collar 1 a leather or metal band put round the neck of an animal.
2 the part of your clothes which fits round the neck.

collect to gather together.

collection a number of things gathered in a set.

college a place where students are taught.

collide to come together with great force.

colonel (say 'kernel') a senior officer in the army.

colour what makes things look green, red, etc.

column 1 a post, usually of stone or wood, used to support a part of a building.
2 a strip of printing in a book or newspaper.
3 a line of troops.

comb a thin piece of metal or plastic with many teeth, used to keep hair tidy.

combine to join or mix together.

comedian a person who tells funny stories in public to make people laugh.

comedy a play or film that makes you laugh.

comfort 1 a pleasant easy feeling.
2 to show kindness to someone in pain or trouble.

comfortable giving or having comfort.

comic 1 which makes you laugh, funny.
2 a magazine or paper for young people with stories told in pictures.

comma a punctuation mark shaped like this **,**

command order.

commercial 1 to do with buying and selling.
2 an advertisement on television etc.

common ordinary, usual; found in many places.

companion someone who is with you, often a friend.

company 1 people you are with.
2 a group of people doing business, a firm.

compare to see if things are alike.

compartment a separate section (for example of a railway carriage or a refrigerator).

compass an instrument which tells you where north is.

compel to force.

competition a contest to find the best.

complain to find fault, to grumble.

complete 1 the whole with nothing missing.
2 to finish altogether.

complicated	having a lot of parts; difficult to understand, not simple.
compliment	something nice someone says to praise you.
composer	a person who makes up music.
computer	a machine that stores information and can work things out quickly.
conceal	to hide from.
conceited	thinking too much of yourself, too proud.
concentrate	to think hard about something.
concern	1 to be connected with. 2 **concerned** worried.
concert	music played in front of an audience.
concise	1 brief, short. 2 in a few words.
conclusion	the finish, the end.
condition	the state of something or someone.
conduct	behaviour.
conduct	to guide, to lead.
conductor	1 a person who is in charge of an orchestra or choir. 2 a person who sells tickets and looks after the passengers on a bus.
cone	1 the fruit of the fir tree. 2 a solid shape that is round at the bottom and pointed at the top, like an ice-cream cornet.
confess	to tell about things you have done wrong.
confident	feeling sure or safe.
confused	not in a clear state of mind; mixed up.
congratulate	to say you are pleased about something good that has happened to someone.
conjuror	a magician, someone who can do tricks.
connect	to join together.
conquer	to beat others in a battle.
conscience	the feeling inside you which tells you if something is right or wrong.
conscious	awake, knowing what is happening.
consent	to agree.
consider	to think carefully.
consonant	a written letter which is not **a**, **e**, **i**, **o**, or **u**.
constable	an ordinary policeman or policewoman.
construct	to build.
contact lens	a small piece of plastic worn on the eye to help you to see better.
contain	to have inside, to hold.
container	a box, jar, chest or bag in which things may be stored.
content	quite pleased, satisfied with things as they are.
contents	what something contains.

contest	a competition to find the best or the winner.	**cork**	1 a light substance made from the bark of the cork tree.
continent	one of the large land masses of the world, such as Europe, Asia or Africa.		2 a piece of this or other substance used to close the mouth of a bottle.
continue	to go on with, to go on, to last.	**corn**	1 the seeds of grain used as food.
control	to guide; to keep steady.		2 a sore, hard place on the foot.
convenient	suitable.	**corner**	where two roads, lines or walls meet.
convent	the building in which nuns live.	**corpse**	a dead body.
conversation	talk between two or more people.	**correct**	1 quite right, true.
			2 to make something right.
convict	a criminal in prison.	**corridor**	a narrow, covered passage which joins rooms, railway compartments, etc.
convict	to find (someone) guilty of a crime in a court.		
convince	to make (someone) believe something.	**cost**	how much you must pay to buy something.
cook	to make food ready to eat by heating it (for example by boiling or frying).	**costume**	clothes worn for a special reason or occasion (for example on the stage).
cool	not quite cold.	**cosy**	1 comfortable and warm.
copper	1 a reddish-brown metal.		2 a cover for a teapot etc.
	2 the colour of this.	**cot**	a baby's bed with high sides.
copy	1 to do the same as somebody else, to imitate.	**cottage**	a small country house.
	2 to make (something) the same as something else.	**cotton**	1 a kind of light cloth made from a plant grown in warm countries.
			2 thread used for sewing.
cord	a piece of thick string or thin rope.	**couch**	a seat for more than one person, a sofa.
core	the part in the centre of something (for example of an apple, where the seeds are).	**cough**	to force air from the chest and lungs with a noise.

council	a group of people chosen to plan and decide what should be done in a place (for example a town or district).	**cousin**	the child of an uncle or aunt.
		cover	to put something over something else.
count	1 to number in the proper order, to add up. 2 a foreign nobleman.	**cow**	1 a large female animal kept for its milk and meat. 2 the female of some other animals (for example the elephant or the whale).
counter	1 a table over which things are served in a shop. 2 a small disc used in counting and in playing games.		
		coward	a person who runs away from danger or difficulty.
countess	a noblewoman, the wife or widow of an earl or a count.	**cowboy**	a man who rides a horse and looks after cattle in America.
country	1 the whole of a land, such as England or France. 2 the part of a land which is away from towns.	**crab**	a kind of shellfish with ten legs.
		crack	1 to break, to make a slight break in. 2 to make a sharp noise like something hard breaking.
county	a division of England, Wales or Ireland.		
couple	two of anything.	**cradle**	a rocking bed for a baby.
coupon	a ticket which can be changed for something of value.	**craft**	a job or trade needing skill, especially with the hands.
courage	great bravery.	**crafty**	not able to be trusted, cunning.
course	1 a large stretch of land where certain sports take place. 2 a part of a meal. 3 the direction something takes.	**crane**	1 a tall machine for lifting heavy things. 2 a large water-bird with long legs.
		crash	1 a loud noise made by something breaking. 2 an accident when cars (for example) bang into something.
court	1 a piece of ground on which certain games are played (for example a **tennis-court**). 2 a place where trials are held. 3 the place where a king and queen live and the people who help them.		
		crawl	1 to move on the hands and knees. 2 to move slowly. 3 a stroke used in swimming.

crayon	a stick of coloured wax for drawing with, a coloured pencil.
crazy	1 mad, without sense. 2 likely to do strange or silly things.
cream	1 the thick liquid found on the top of milk. 2 the colour of cream.
crease	1 the mark made by folding cloth, for example. 2 a mark on a cricket pitch.
create	to make something new.
creature	any living thing.
credit	1 good name, honour. 2 buying things to pay for them later.
creep	1 to move along close to the ground. 2 to move carefully, often to avoid being seen.
crescent	1 part of the edge of a circle; the shape of the new moon. 2 a curved street.
crest	1 the top of something, especially the top of a wave. 2 feathers on the top of something.
crew	a team of people who do the work on a ship or an aircraft etc.
cricket	1 a game played with a ball, bat and stumps. 2 a jumping insect which chirps.
crime	breaking the law.
criminal	a person who breaks the law.
crimson	a deep red colour.
cripple	a person who cannot fully use an arm or a leg.
crisis	a time when something serious or dangerous happens.
crisp	1 firm and dry. 2 a very thin slice of potato cooked in oil.
crockery	plates, cups, etc.
crocodile	a large and dangerous animal found in some hot countries, especially in rivers.
crocus	a small yellow, purple or white spring flower.
crook	1 a person who commits a crime, a criminal. 2 a shepherd's stick with a hook at one end.
crooked	1 bent, not straight. 2 dishonest.
crop	1 plants grown for food. 2 the amount of such gathered at one time.
cross	1 anything shaped like a × or +. 2 to move from one side to the other. 3 angry.
crouch	to bend down low with your legs bent.
crow	a kind of large, black bird which has a loud, rough cry.
crowd	a large number of people all together in one place.

crown	1 the special head-dress, often made of gold, of a king or queen. 2 the top of something such as a person's head or a hill.
cruel	very unkind, without pity.
cruise	a long journey by boat or aeroplane.
crumb	a tiny piece of bread or cake.
crumble	to break into little pieces.
crush	to press together very tightly, to squash.
crust	the hard outside part of anything, especially of bread.
crutch	a wood or metal support used by someone with a hurt leg to help them walk.
cry	1 to call out. 2 to have tears in your eyes, to weep.
cub	a young fox, wolf, lion, etc.
cube	a solid, square shape.
cuckoo	a bird which lays its eggs in other birds' nests and makes a sound like this word.
cucumber	a long, green vegetable often eaten in salads.
cuddle	to take into the arms and hug closely.
cuff	the end of a sleeve.
culprit	a person who is guilty of doing wrong, the person to blame.

cultivate	to dig or plough land so that crops will grow.
cunning	clever in a sly way.
cupboard	a place with shelves for storing things.
cure	to make somebody better after an illness.
curious	1 strange, unusual. 2 wanting to know.
curls	hair formed into rings.
currant	1 a small, dried grape often used in puddings and cakes. 2 a small berry grown on a bush.
current	a flow of water, air, electricity, etc.
curry	a food with a hot taste.
curtain	a cloth which hangs in front of or beside a window or a stage.
curve	a smooth, round shape, a smooth bend.
cushion	a pillow which is often used on a chair.
custard	a sweet, yellow sauce which is eaten with puddings.
custom	what is usually done; what usually happens.
customer	a person who buys something in a shop or market.
cut	to open or to divide with something sharp.
cutlery	knives, forks and spoons.

cycle	1 a bicycle. 2 to make a bicycle move.
cylinder	a long, round, solid shape, like a soup tin.

D d

dab	to touch lightly.
daffodil	a yellow spring flower grown from a bulb.
dagger	a pointed knife with a short blade, sharp on both sides.
daily	each day.
dairy	1 a place where butter and cheese are made from milk and cream; a place where milk is put into bottles. 2 a shop where milk, butter, eggs and cheese are sold.
daisy	a small flower with a yellow centre and white petals.
dam	a wall built to hold back water.
damage	to harm.
damp	slightly wet.
damson	a small, dark-purple plum.
dance	to move on the feet to music.
dandelion	a yellow wild flower.
danger	harm; something that can hurt you.
dangerous	likely to hurt, harm or kill.

dangle	to hang down from something, to swing loosely from something.
dare	1 to be brave enough to do something dangerous. 2 to ask (someone) to do something dangerous.
dark	not light or bright.
darling	a name for someone you love very much.
dart	1 to move very quickly. 2 a small arrow thrown at a board in a game.
dash	1 to rush from place to place. 2 a short line like this — used in writing.
date	1 the day, month and year when something takes place. 2 a sweet, brown fruit.
daughter	a female child of a parent.
dawdle	to do something so slowly that time is wasted.
dawn	the very first light of the day, daybreak.
day	1 a period of twenty-four hours. 2 the time between sunrise and sunset.
dazed	not knowing where you are (for example after a blow on the head).
dazzle	to blind for a moment with bright light.
dead	no longer alive.

deadly	able to cause death.
deaf	not able to hear (well).
deal	1 to do business with. 2 to give out (cards) in a card game. **a great deal** a lot. **deal with** to do what has to be done with.
dear	1 much loved by someone. 2 costing a lot of money.
death	when you stop living.
debt	what you owe to someone.
deceive	to fool someone by telling them lies.
decent	proper, respectable.
decide	to make up your mind about something.
decimal	a way of counting in tens.
decision	what you have decided.
deck	the floor of a boat, an aeroplane or a bus.
declare	to state firmly, to say what you intend to do.
decorate	1 to paint or wallpaper a room or a house. 2 to make something more attractive, usually with ornaments etc.
decrease	to make smaller.
deed	an action, something done.
deep	far down, often in water; far inside.
deer	a large, fast-running wild animal.

defeat	to beat in battle or in a game.
defend	to protect, to guard.
definite	sure, certain.
defy	to refuse openly to do what you are told; to refuse to obey (an order).
degree	a measurement of heat or of an angle.
delay	1 to put off doing something for a while. 2 to make late.
deliberate	done on purpose.
delicate	very fine; easily broken.
delicious	having a very pleasant taste or smell.
delight	great pleasure, joy.
deliver	to bring, to carry.
demand	to ask very firmly for something.
demonstrate	to show clearly to other people how something should be done.
den	the place where a wild animal eats and sleeps.
denim	strong, usually blue, cotton cloth.
dense	very thick, too thick to see through.
dent	a hollow caused by a blow or knock.
dentist	a person who looks after teeth.
deny	to say firmly that something is not true.
departure	the moment of leaving or going away.

depend	to trust somebody or something for help.	**destruction**	the act of destroying or breaking down completely.
depress	to make (someone) feel sad.	**detail**	a very small part or fact.
depth	how deep something is.	**detective**	a person, usually a policeman, whose job it is to find out who carried out a crime.
descend	to go down; to come down.		
describe	to say how something or someone looks.	**detergent**	a kind of soap for washing clothes or dishes, for example.
description	saying what something is.	**detest**	to dislike greatly, to hate.
desert	a large, empty place where hardly anything grows because of heat and lack of water.	**develop**	1 to grow, to change gradually. 2 to bring out the picture in a photographic film.
desert	to leave when you are expected to stay.	**device**	a useful object or plan for doing something.
deserve	to be worthy of, to have earned some reward or punishment.	**dew**	drops of water found on the ground and on plants in the early morning.
design	a plan or drawing; a pattern.	**diagram**	a drawing to show how something works or is made.
desire	to want something very much.	**dial**	the face of an object such as a clock or telephone, with numbers or letters on it.
desk	a kind of table used for writing at.		
despair	to lose hope; to give up hope.	**dialect**	how people speak in a certain district.
desperate	ready to do almost anything to get what you want, because you have lost hope.	**diamond**	1 a very hard precious stone, often used in rings. 2 a shape with four sloping sides that are the same length. 3 one of the four kinds in a pack of playing cards.
dessert (say 'de<u>sert</u>')	the sweet dish eaten at the end of a meal.		
destination	the place you are going to or to which something has been sent.		
destroy	to break up completely, to do away with.	**diary**	a book in which you write what happens each day.

dice	a small, square block with spots on it, used in many games.
dictate	1 to tell others what to do. 2 to say something for someone else to write down.
dictionary	a book like this one with a list of words and their meanings, arranged in alphabetical order.
die	to stop living.
diet	1 the sort of food we eat. 2 an eating plan to let you lose weight or be healthier.
difference	what makes something different.
different	not like something else, not the same.
difficult	not easy to do or to understand.
dig	to turn soil over.
digest	to break down food in your stomach after you have eaten it.
dim	not bright; not easy to see.
din	a great noise of many things together.
dinghy	a small rowing-boat.
dinner	the main meal of the day.
dip	1 to place into a liquid for a short time. 2 to slope downwards.
direct	1 the shortest and quickest way. 2 to tell (somebody) which way to go.

dirt	mud, dust, something not clean.
dirty	not clean.
disabled	not able to use part of your body properly.
disagree	not to agree with.
disappear	to go out of sight, to vanish.
disappoint	to make (somebody) sorry because they have not got what they hoped for.
disaster	a terrible event, happening or accident.
disc also spelt **disk**	1 a round, flat object. 2 a plastic **disk** for storing information in a computer.
disco	a place where people dance to music on records.
discover	to find out about (something); to find for the first time.
discuss	to talk about (something) with other people.
disease	an illness.
disgraceful	so bad you should be ashamed of it.
disguise	to change your appearance by altering your face and clothes.
disgust	strong feeling against something.
dish	1 a bowl or plate. 2 food served at a meal.
dishonest	not honest or trustworthy.
disk	see **disc**.

dislike	not to like.
dismal	dull or sad, not bright.
dismiss	to send (someone) away.
display	a show.
dissolve	to mix completely with a liquid.
distance	1 somewhere far away. 2 the space between two points or places.
distinct	1 quite clearly seen or heard. 2 different.
distress	great trouble, sorrow or unhappiness.
district	a part of a country or a town.
disturb	1 to upset, to worry. 2 to put out of order.
disturbance	trouble; an upset.
ditch	a long, narrow hole dug in the ground (for example to let water flow away).
dive	to jump head first into water.
diver	someone wearing special equipment who works under water.
divide	1 to share between; to split up. 2 to work out how many times one number goes into another.
dizzy	unsteady, feeling as though you are spinning round.

dock	1 the place where boats are loaded and unloaded. 2 the place where a prisoner stands in a court of law.
doctor	a person who looks after people's health.
dodge	to move quickly from one side to the other; to avoid.
doe	a female deer or rabbit.
doll	a toy which looks like a baby or child.
dollar	a form of money used in some countries, such as America or Canada.
dolphin	a warm-blooded sea animal.
dome	a rounded roof of a large building such as a church.
domino	an oblong piece of wood or plastic with dots on it, used in the game of **dominoes.**
donkey	an animal like a small horse with very long ears.
door	an entrance to a room or a building.
dormitory	a large room containing several beds.
dose	the amount of medicine that you should take at one time.
dot	a tiny, round mark or point.
double	twice the amount.
doubt	not to be sure, to question.

dough	a soft mixture of flour and water etc.
dove	a kind of pigeon, often white.
down	1 lower; below. 2 soft hair or feathers.
doze	to sleep lightly.
dozen	12, twelve.
drag	to pull something along the ground.
dragon	an imaginary, fire-breathing animal in stories.
dragonfly	a long insect with fine wings.
drain	to take water away from something.
drains	the pipes which take the dirty water from buildings.
drama	1 stories that can be acted, plays. 2 an exciting happening.
draught	a cold stream of air entering a warmer room.
draughts	a game played with round pieces on a board with black and white squares.
draw	1 to make a picture, usually with a pen and pencil. 2 to pull. 3 to end a game with equal scores.
drawer	a box with handles that fits closely into a piece of furniture.
dreadful	very bad, terrible.
dream	to see and hear things when you are asleep.
drench	to soak through with water.
dress	1 to put on your clothes. 2 a woman's or girl's garment like a skirt and blouse together. 3 to clean and cover (a wound).
drift	1 snow blown into a deep pile. 2 to move aimlessly with the tide or with the wind.
drill	1 a tool for making holes. 2 to make a hole. 3 exercises (for example for soldiers).
drink	to swallow liquids.
drip	to fall or let fall in drops.
drive	1 to make a vehicle, such as a car, or an animal move. 2 a private road up to a house.
drizzle	light rain falling gently.
droop	to hang down loosely.
drop	1 one tiny spot of liquid. 2 to fall from a height.
drought (rhymes with 'out')	a long time when no rain falls and there is not enough water.
drown	to die in water because you cannot breathe.
drug	1 a substance used as a medicine. 2 a substance used to make you feel different (for example alcohol).

drum	a musical instrument which is played by beating it with a stick.
dry	not wet or damp.
duchess	a noblewoman of high rank, the wife or widow of a duke.
duck	1 a common water bird. 2 to bend down quickly (for example so as not to be hit).
duel	a fight between two people armed with the same sort of weapons.
duet	a song or a piece of music for two people.
duke	a nobleman of high rank.
dull	1 not shining. 2 not clever.
dumb	unable to speak.
dump	1 a place where things are stored roughly or thrown away. 2 to put (something) down heavily or carelessly.
dungeon	a prison below the ground.
during	as long as something lasts.
dusk	the beginning of darkness just after sunset, the half-dark.
dust	tiny specks of dirt.
duster	a cloth to remove dust.
duty	something that you should do.
duvet (say '<u>doo</u>vay')	a padded bed cover.

dwarf	a person or an animal much smaller than usual.
dwell	to live in a certain place.
dye	to make something a certain colour by placing it in a special liquid.

E e

each	every one by itself.
eager	very keen.
eagle	a large, wild bird which kills small animals for food.
ear	1 the part of the head with which we hear. 2 where the seed is found in the corn plant.
earl	a nobleman.
early	1 before the time fixed. 2 near the beginning.
earn	1 to get money etc. by working. 2 to deserve.
earth	1 the world in which we live. 2 the soil in which things grow.
earthquake	when part of the earth's surface shakes.
earwig	a small insect.
east	the direction from which the sun rises.
easy	simple to do, not difficult to understand.

eat	to bite, chew and swallow food.	**elder**	1 the older one of two persons. 2 a tree with white flowers and black berries.
echo	the same sound which comes back to you in an empty place.	**election**	choosing someone by a vote.
edge	the rim, the border.	**electric**	using electricity.
editor	1 the person in charge of a newspaper or magazine. 2 a person who prepares a book or a paper for printing, or who prepares a film or a video for showing.	**electricity**	a power for heating, lighting, driving things, etc. which goes through wires.
		elephant	a very large animal with a trunk and two tusks, found in Africa and India.
education	learning and teaching, especially in schools, colleges and universities.	**eleven**	11, a number.
eel	a snake-like fish.	**elf**	a kind of small fairy.
effect	what happens because of something.	**elm**	a kind of large tree.
effort	the use of all your strength in trying to do something.	**embarrass**	to make (someone) feel uncomfortable.
		embrace	to put your arms round someone lovingly, to hug.
e.g.	for example.	**embroider**	to sew patterns on cloth.
egg	the rounded object from which some creatures, for example fish and birds, are hatched.	**emerald**	1 a bright-green precious stone. 2 the colour of this.
eight	8, a number.	**emergency**	something very bad which needs to be dealt with right away.
eighteen	18, a number.		
eighty	80, a number.	**emigrate**	to leave one country to go to live in another.
either	one or the other (of two people or things).	**emotion**	something you feel strongly, such as anger or love.
elastic	a material that will stretch and then go back to its own length.	**emperor**	a man who is the head of a number of countries.
elbow	the joint in the middle of the arm.	**empire**	many countries which are all under the same ruler.

employ	to give paid work to (someone).	**enough**	as many or as much as needed.
empress	a woman who is the head of a number of countries; the wife of an emperor.	**enquire**	to ask questions.
		enter	to go into or to come into.
empty	with nothing at all inside.	**entertain**	to put people in a good mood by doing something for them.
enamel	1 a special kind of hard, shiny paint. 2 the hard covering on your teeth.		
		entertainment	something which is done to give pleasure to people.
enclose	1 to place inside. 2 to surround by a fence or wall.	**enthusiastic**	very keen, very interested.
		entire	the whole thing, complete.
encourage	to act or speak in a way which helps someone to do something.	**entrance**	the place where you enter, the way in.
encyclopedia	a book containing facts about a lot of different things.	**entry**	1 going or coming in. 2 an entrance.
end	1 the last part of something. 2 to finish.	**envelope**	the cover in which a letter is placed.
		envy	to wish you could have what somebody else has.
enemy	someone you fight against.	**equal**	1 exactly the same as. 2 just as good as.
energy	power, strength to do things.	**equator**	an imaginary line round the earth half-way between the North and South Poles.
engaged	1 going to be married. 2 being used by someone else.		
engine	a machine driven by some sort of power which makes things move.	**equipment**	the things you need to do something.
		erect	1 perfectly upright. 2 to build.
engineer	someone who plans or looks after machines, roads, buildings, bridges, etc.	**errand**	a short journey to take a message or to fetch something.
enjoy	to like doing something very much.	**error**	a mistake.
enormous	very large.	**escape**	to get away, to find a way out.

especially	very, more than usual.
essay	a piece of writing on a particular subject.
essential	needed, (something) which you must have.
estate	1 a large piece of land belonging to one person. 2 a number of houses and shops built in one place.
estimate	to guess the size or price of (something).
etc.	and so on.
eternal	lasting for ever.
even	1 flat and smooth. 2 (of a number) that can be divided by two, not odd: 4, 6, 8, etc. are **even** numbers.
evening	the time between afternoon and night.
event	1 a happening, especially an important one. 2 an item on a sports programme.
eventually	at last, in the end.
ever	always, at all times.
evergreen	a plant that does not lose its leaves in the winter.
every	each one of many.
evident	easy to see, plain.
evil	very bad, very wicked.
ewe (say 'you')	a female sheep.
exact	absolutely correct, quite right.

exaggerate	to say more than is really true.
examination	a test of how good someone or something is in a particular way, a check.
example	1 one thing taken out of a number of things to show what the rest are like. 2 good behaviour you should copy.
excellent	very good.
exchange	1 to change for something else. 2 a building where telephone lines are connected.
excite	to give strong and often pleasant feelings.
exclaim	to shout out suddenly.
excursion	a journey for pleasure.
excuse (rhymes with 'loose')	a reason for not doing what you should have done.
excuse (rhymes with 'news')	to forgive.
execute	to put to death.
exercise	movement such as walking, running, etc. to keep you fit.
exhibition	a display, a show (for example of pictures).
exist	to live; to be.
exit	the way out of a place.
expand	to grow larger, to spread out.

expect	to think something will happen.
expedition	a special journey to a place to find out more about it.
expel	to send away; to drive out.
expensive	costing a lot of money.
experiment	a test done on something to find out more about it.
expert	a person who is very good at something or knows a lot about something.
explain	to say clearly how something happened or what something is about.
explode	to burst or blow up with a loud noise.
explore	to search a place thoroughly to find out more about it.
export	to send goods out of a country.
express	1 to state clearly. 2 travelling more quickly than usual.
extend	to stretch out, to make larger.
extra	1 in addition to. 2 more than is needed or usual.
extraordinary	very strange, unusual.
extreme	1 farthest away. 2 very great indeed.
eye	1 the part of the head with which you see. 2 the hole in a needle.

F f

fable	a story or legend, often about animals, which teaches you something.
face	1 the front part of the head. 2 the front of an object. 3 to turn towards something.
fact	something that is true.
factory	a place where goods are made by machinery.
fade	1 to lose colour, to become dim. 2 to begin to grow weaker.
fail	1 not to do something that you are expected to do. 2 not to pass an exam.
faint	1 not clear, not easy to see. 2 to lose one's senses, become unconscious.
fair	1 light in colour, not dark, blonde. 2 reasonable, just. 3 an open-air entertainment; a market. 4 neither good nor bad, quite good.
fairy	an imaginary person with magic power.
faith	belief in somebody or something.
faithful	true; able to be trusted.
fall	to drop, come down; to become lower.

false	1 not true; not real. 2 not able to be trusted.
familiar	well-known to you.
family	a group of close relatives, especially a father, a mother and their children.
famine	being without food for a very long time.
famous	well known because of what you have done.
fan	1 an instrument to make air move and keep you cool. 2 a person who takes a great interest for example in a football team or a pop singer.
fancy	1 to think that you can see something. 2 decorated, not plain. 3 to want.
fang	a long, sharp tooth on some animals and snakes.
far	not near, a long way away.
fare	money paid for a journey.
farm	land (usually with a house and other buildings) used for growing crops and keeping animals.
farmer	a person who owns or looks after a farm.
farther	at a greater distance away.
fashion	up-to-date dress and style.

fast	1 very quick, at great speed. 2 a time without food. 3 stopped from moving.
fasten	to tie or join things together.
fat	1 very big all round, not thin. 2 the greasy part of meat.
fatal	causing death.
fate	what is going to happen or is likely to happen in the future.
father	a male parent.
fault	1 something which is not right and which spoils a thing or person. 2 a mistake, something you do wrong.
favour	something good you do for someone.
favourite	the one that you like better than any of the others.
fawn	1 a young deer. 2 a light-brown colour.
fear	to be afraid of; to be frightened that something might happen.
feast	a large special meal; a banquet.
feather	one of the flat, light things which cover a bird's body and wings.
feeble	weak, with no strength.
feed	to give food to.
feel	1 to know something by touching it. 2 to think.

fellow	a man or boy, a person.
felt	thick, woolly cloth.
female	a girl or a woman; an animal which can be a mother.
feminine	concerning girls or women.
fence	1 a wood or metal barrier (for example round a field or garden). 2 to fight with swords as a sport.
fern	a plant with feathery leaves but no flowers.
ferret	a small, furry animal used for hunting rabbits.
ferry	a boat which carries people and cars across water.
festival	a special occasion for large numbers of people to enjoy themselves.
fetch	to go and get, to bring back what you were sent for.
fever	an illness which makes the body hot.
few	not many.
fibre	thread-like substance usually used to make into something.
fiddle	a violin.
fidget	to be restless; to wriggle about.
field	a piece of land that is usually enclosed by a hedge, fence or wall.

fierce	violent, wild, cruel.
fifteen	15, a number.
fifty	50, a number.
fig	a sweet fruit full of tiny seeds.
fight	a struggle or battle between two or more people.
figure	1 number used in mathematics. 2 a shape, especially of the human body.
file	1 an instrument with a rough edge for making things smooth. 2 a line of people one behind the other. 3 a box or folder for keeping papers in an office.
fill	to make full.
film	1 a very thin covering. 2 a roll put into a camera to take photographs. 3 a story shown in a cinema or on television.
filthy	very dirty.
fin	one of the thin, flat parts of a fish which help it to swim.
final	1 the end, the last. 2 the last match in a competition, which decides the winner.
finch	a kind of small bird.
find	to come across something you have been looking for.

fine	1 when the weather is pleasant.
	2 very good, excellent.
	3 very thin.
	4 a sum of money paid as a punishment for breaking the law.
finger	one of the five long parts of the hand.
finish	to complete, to end.
fir	an evergreen tree with cones.
fire	1 things burning.
	2 to shoot a gun.
fireman	a person whose job it is to prevent or put out fires.
firework	a tube with gunpowder in it which makes a display of coloured flames and sparks when lit.
firm	1 without changing; fixed.
	2 a group of people running a business.
first	1 at the very beginning.
	2 coming before everyone else (for example in a race).
first aid	giving help to someone who is injured or ill before a doctor comes.
fish	1 an animal which lives and breathes in water.
	2 to try to catch fish.
fisherman	a person who catches fish.
fishmonger	a person who sells fish in a shop.
fist	the hand and fingers closed tightly together.

fit	1 in good health, well and strong.
	2 suitable.
	3 to be the right size for.
five	5, a number.
fix	1 to put in place firmly.
	2 to put right.
fizzy	with a lot of bubbles.
flag	a piece of cloth with a special pattern and colours, the sign of a country or club.
flake	a small, thin piece of something.
flame	the bright, blazing part of a fire.
flap	1 a piece that hangs down or over something.
	2 the up and down movement of a bird's wings, for example.
flare	to blaze up suddenly.
flash	a beam of light which comes and goes quickly.
flask	1 a container for keeping things hot.
	2 a narrow-necked bottle.
flat	1 level.
	2 a set of rooms all on one floor.
	3 below the correct note in music.
flatter	to say that someone is better than they really are.
flavour	the taste of something.

flaw	a fault, a weak place.
flea	a tiny jumping insect which bites people and animals.
flee	to go away quickly; to run from trouble or danger.
fleece	the wool of a sheep or a goat.
fleet	a number of ships together.
flesh	the soft part of the body which covers the bones.
flight	1 flying. 2 escaping.
fling	to throw something away from you.
flint	a kind of very hard stone.
float	to stay on the surface of water without sinking.
flock	1 a number of animals of the same sort together. 2 to gather together.
flood	when water overflows from rivers and lakes onto roads and fields.
floor	the part of a room you walk on.
florist	a person who sells flowers.
flour	wheat which has been crushed into a powder which is used for baking.
flow	to move smoothly along like running water.
flower	the part of a plant, usually colourful, which produces the seeds.

flu	an illness like a very bad cold which causes shivering and aches all over the body.
fluff	small, soft pieces of cloth etc. which can fly about and catch dust.
flute	a high-pitched metal or wood musical instrument played by blowing.
flutter	the quick movement of a bird's wings, for example.
fly	1 to move through the air, especially on wings or in an aircraft. 2 a kind of small insect with wings.
foal	a young horse.
foam	bubbles on the top of a liquid.
fog	air which is thick with mist and smoke.
fold	to bend (paper or clothes, for example) so that one part covers another.
folder	a cardboard cover for papers etc.
folk	people.
follow	1 to go after; to come after. 2 to be able to understand something you heard or read.
fond	**to be fond of somebody** to like them very much.
food	what people, animals and plants take in to keep them alive.

fool
1 a person who behaves in a silly way.
2 to trick somebody.

foolish
slightly stupid, silly.

foot
1 the part of the leg you stand on.
2 a measure of length equal to twelve inches.

footwear
things worn on the feet (for example boots, shoes and socks).

forbid
to tell somebody not to do something.

force
1 strength, power.
2 to make somebody do something.

forecast
to say what is likely to happen.

forehead
the part of the head between the hair and the eyes.

foreign
belonging to another country.

forest
a large area of woodland.

forge
1 to copy someone's writing, painting or signature, usually for a bad reason.
2 a blacksmith's workshop.

forget
1 not to remember.
2 to leave (something) behind.

fork
1 a small tool with long, thin spikes for eating with.
2 a large tool with long, thin spikes for digging and lifting things.
3 where two roads or rivers meet.

form
1 the shape of something.
2 a printed paper with spaces for you to write things in.
3 a class in a school.

fort
a strong building to protect people from attack.

fortnight
a period of two weeks.

fortunate
lucky.

fortune
1 good or bad luck.
2 a lot of money.

forty
40, a number.

forward
towards the front.

fossil
the mark or remains of a creature or plant found in rocks.

foster
to bring up a child who is not your own.

foul
1 very dirty or bad.
2 something that is against the rules (for example in a sport).

found
to start something such as a hospital or a school.

fountain
a device for throwing a thin stream of water into the air.

four
4, a number.

fourteen
14, a number.

fowl
a bird, especially one kept for its meat and eggs.

fox
a wild animal like a dog with a reddish-brown coat and a long, thick tail.

fraction
a part of something.

fragment	a small piece from something larger.
frame	a border placed round a picture.
freckle	one of the tiny, light -brown marks found on the skin of some people.
free	1 able to do as you wish. 2 given away for nothing.
freeze	to make or be very hard and cold; to turn into ice.
frequent	happening often.
fresh	1 new; newly gathered; not kept too long; (of food) not tinned. 2 not tired. 3 (of water) not salt.
fridge	short for **refrigerator.**
friend	somebody you like and can trust and like doing things with.
fright	sudden fear.
frill	a decoration round the edge.
fringe	1 short hair brushed forward over the forehead. 2 a border of loose threads, used to decorate a rug or a lampshade, for example.
frisky	lively, jumping with pleasure.
frock	a dress.
frog	a small jumping animal which can live on land and in water.

front	the part opposite the back, the beginning of something.
frost	1 white, powdery ice seen in very cold weather. 2 very cold, freezing weather.
froth	bubbles on top of a liquid, foam.
frown	to wrinkle the forehead, to show you are annoyed or puzzled.
frozen	very cold; made into ice.
fruit	the part of certain plants where the seeds are found; many kinds are good to eat (for example strawberries, oranges).
fry	to cook in boiling fat or oil in a pan.
fudge	a kind of soft, brown toffee.
fuel	anything that can be burned to give heat or light.
full	unable to hold anything more.
fun	something enjoyable, amusement, lively pleasure.
fund	a collection of money for something special.
funeral	the ceremony held when someone dies.
funnel	1 the chimney on a ship or an engine. 2 a tube with a wide mouth (used for example to pour liquids into bottles).

funny	*1* amusing, making you laugh. *2* strange, odd.
fur	the soft, hairy covering of some animals.
furious	very angry.
furnace	a covered fire to melt metals.
furniture	chairs, tables and similar things.
further	at a greater distance, beyond.
fuse	*1* a piece of material which is lit to set off an explosion or a firework. *2* part of an electric plug or system.
fuss	an excited state, usually about something quite small.
future	the time yet to come.

G g

gable	the pointed end wall of a building.
gag	to cover the mouth to prevent a person from speaking.
gain	*1* a profit that is made. *2* to get or win something.
gale	a very strong wind.
galleon	(long ago) a Spanish sailing-ship.

gallery	*1* a high platform, often with seats, in a cinema, a theatre, or a church. *2* a building or a large room used for showing pictures.
galley	*1* a ship's kitchen. *2* (long ago) a kind of low sailing-ship with many oars.
gallon	a measure of liquid equal to 8 pints.
gallop	to move very fast on four legs, like a horse.
gamble	to play games for money.
game	*1* something that you play; a sport. *2* wild animals or birds which are hunted for sport or food.
gander	a male goose.
gang	a group of people doing something together.
gangway	*1* a pathway between rows of seats. *2* a bridge placed between a ship and a dock.
gaol (say 'jail')	a prison.
gap	an opening between two objects.
gape	to open wide.
garage	a place where cars etc. are kept or repaired and petrol is sold.
garbage	rubbish, things to be thrown out.

garden	land where flowers, fruit and vegetables are grown.	**gentle**	soft, not rough; full of care for other people.
garment	a piece of clothing.	**gentleman**	1 a man who is well-mannered. 2 a polite word for a man.
gas	1 a substance like air which is neither liquid nor solid. 2 a kind of gas which burns, used for heating and cooking.	**genuine**	real, true.
		geography	knowledge about the earth and its people.
gash	a long, deep cut.	**geology**	knowledge about rocks and how they are made.
gasp	to breathe in very quickly, often in surprise.	**gerbil**	a desert animal like a small rat, often kept as a pet.
gate	a kind of door in a wall or fence.	**germ**	a tiny living thing that often causes illness.
gather	1 to collect together. 2 to pick flowers or other plants.	**ghost**	the spirit of a dead person, believed to be seen moving about.
gay	happy, cheerful.	**giant**	1 a huge man (for example in a fairy story). 2 anything that is much larger than usual.
gaze	to look for a long time; to stare steadily.		
gazelle	a kind of small deer found in Africa and Asia.		
gear	1 a set of wheels with teeth to make an engine turn. 2 what you need with you, for example to play some sports.	**giddy**	dizzy, when everything seems to be going round and round.
		gift	something given, a present.
		giggle	to laugh in a foolish way.
gem	a precious stone which is used for jewellery (for example a diamond).	**gills**	the openings in a fish's head by which it breathes.
general	1 usual; often done. 2 an army officer of high rank.	**ginger**	1 a kind of hot flavouring used in cooking. 2 a reddish-brown colour.
generous	kind; giving away freely.	**giraffe**	an African wild animal with a very long neck and long legs.
genius	a person who is very clever.		

girl
1 a female child.
2 a young woman.

give
to hand over to someone else.

glad
happy, pleased, delighted.

glance
to look at something and then look away quickly.

glare
1 to stare at in anger.
2 unpleasant brightness.

glass
1 a hard material through which you can usually see.
2 a cup without a handle which is made of glass.

glasses
two pieces of special glass put in a light frame and worn to help you to see better.

gleam
to shine faintly.

glide
to move along very smoothly.

glider
a kind of aeroplane that glides through the air without an engine.

glimmer
a faint light which can hardly be seen.

glimpse
a very short look, a glance.

glitter
to throw out bright rays of light, to sparkle.

globe
1 an object like a ball.
2 a round ball with a map of the world drawn on it.

gloomy
1 dark and dismal.
2 sad and serious.

glory
great fame given to someone who has done something very important or valuable.

gloss
brightness on the surface of something.

glove
one of a pair of coverings for the hands with a separate place for each finger.

glow
to shine with a soft light, to burn without flame.

glue
a substance for sticking things together.

glum
looking sad and unhappy.

glutton
a person who eats too much.

gnash
to grind the teeth together because you are angry or in trouble.

gnat
a tiny winged insect which bites.

gnaw
to wear away by using the teeth; to eat by scraping away.

gnome
a dwarf or goblin that is supposed to live under the ground.

go
to move away; to leave.

goal
1 a place you aim at in games such as football and hockey.
2 the score made when the ball goes into goal.

goat
a grass-eating animal which has horns and which gives milk.

gobble
to eat greedily and noisily.

goblin
a kind of wicked fairy.

God
the being who is above all others and to whom people pray.

gold	a yellow precious metal.	**government**	the people who are in charge of a country.
golden	1 looking like gold. 2 made of gold.	**gown**	a dress.
goldfish	a small, bright-orange fish often kept in tanks and ponds.	**grab**	to snatch, to grasp quickly.
		grace	1 a short prayer before or after a meal. 2 a beautiful way of moving.
golf	a game played on a large stretch of land with special clubs and a small ball.	**grade**	1 a level, size, quality. 2 to put into groups (according to size, for example).
good	1 right; true. 2 kind. 3 well-behaved.		
		gradual	little by little.
goodbye	something said when leaving people.	**grain**	1 a tiny piece of sand or soil. 2 the seed of corn. 3 the lines in wood.
goods	things which are bought, sold and owned.		
goose	a bird like a large duck.	**gram**	a small unit of weight.
gooseberry	a green fruit which grows on a small, prickly bush.	**grammar**	the rules of a language.
		grand	very large and fine, splendid.
gorgeous	splendid, magnificent, very beautiful.	**grandfather**	the father of your father or mother.
gorilla	the largest kind of ape.		
gospel	1 teachings of Jesus Christ. 2 one of the first four books of the New Testament.	**grandmother**	the mother of your father or mother.
		granite	a very hard rock often used for buildings and monuments.
gossip	1 to talk for a long time about unimportant things, often about other people. 2 a person who tells usually hurtful stories about other people.	**grant**	to give; to allow.
		grape	a small, juicy fruit with green or purple skin.
		grapefruit	a yellow fruit like a large orange.
govern	to be in control of, to rule over (a country, for example).	**grasp**	1 to hold firmly in the hand. 2 to understand what you have been told.

grass	the common green plant used to feed animals and to cover parks and gardens.	**green**	1 the colour of grass. 2 an area of grass.
grasshopper	an insect with strong back legs for jumping.	**greenhouse**	a building with glass walls and roof in which plants are grown.
grate	1 where the fire burns in a fireplace. 2 to rub something into little pieces using a rough surface.	**greet**	to welcome with words and actions.
grateful	thankful, feeling gratitude.	**grey**	a colour half-way between black and white.
		grief	sorrow, deep sadness.
grater	an instrument with jagged points used to grate cheese, for example.	**grill**	a part of a cooker using overhead direct heat.
		grim	stern; severe; fierce.
gratitude	warm feelings towards someone who has been helpful or kind.	**grin**	a wide smile.
		grind	1 to rub something until it becomes powder. 2 to sharpen (a tool, for example) by rubbing the edge.
grave	1 a burial place in the ground. 2 serious.		
		grip	to grasp tightly.
gravel	small pieces of stone.	**groan**	to make a low, sad sound, usually when hurt.
gravity	the force which pulls objects towards the earth.	**grocer**	a person who sells foods and other goods for the house.
gravy	a brown liquid eaten with meat, often made from the juice of the meat.	**groom**	1 a person who looks after horses. 2 to brush and clean a horse. 3 short for **bridegroom.**
graze	1 to rub away the skin. 2 to feed from grass.		
grease	1 animal fat. 2 thick oil used to make machinery run smoothly.		
		groove	a narrow channel cut into something.
		ground	1 the surface of the earth; land. 2 a place for playing certain outdoor games.
great	1 big. 2 important. 3 very good.		
greedy	always wanting more; never satisfied.	**group**	a number of people, animals or things together.

grouse
1 a plump game bird found especially on the Scottish moors.
2 to complain, grumble.

grow
1 to become bigger.
2 to raise plants.

growl
to show anger by snarling, like a dog.

grub
an insect, such as a caterpillar, before it has grown wings or legs.

grubby
dirty.

gruff
having a rough, coarse voice.

grumble
to complain, not loudly but often.

grunt
a noise like that made by a pig.

guard
1 to keep safe.
2 a person whose job it is to protect something or someone.
3 a person in charge of a train on its journey.

guardian
someone who looks after another person especially when taking the place of a parent.

guerrilla
a person who fights secretly against the people in power.

guess
to say what you think is correct without really knowing.

guest
1 a visitor to someone's house.
2 a person staying in a hotel.

guide
a person who shows the way.

guilt
1 having done wrong.
2 the feeling of having done wrong.

guitar
a musical instrument with six strings, played by plucking the strings.

gulf
a large bay.

gull
a kind of common sea-bird.

gulp
to swallow greedily and noisily.

gum
1 a substance used to stick things together.
2 the part of the mouth round the roots of the teeth.
3 chewing gum; a chewy sweet.

gun
a weapon from which bullets are fired.

gurgle
to make a bubbling noise like water leaving a container.

gush
to flow out quickly in large amounts.

gust
a sudden wind.

gutter
a channel for water along the edge of a road or roof, for example.

guy
1 a model of Guy Fawkes, burnt on a bonfire on 5 November.
2 a man.

gymnastics
exercises for the body.

gypsy
a member of a tribe of wandering people.

H h

habit
something you do a lot without thinking about it much, a custom.

haddock
a sea-fish used as food.

haggard
looking tired, thin and ill.

hail
1 frozen raindrops.
2 to call to someone, to greet.

hair
a thread-like covering which grows on the head and the skins of people and animals.

hairdresser
a person who cuts and arranges hair.

half
one of two equal parts of a thing.

hall
1 a very large room for meetings.
2 an entrance passage.
3 a very large house.

halo
1 a ring of light round the sun or moon.
2 a circle painted or drawn round the heads of holy people in pictures.

halt
to stop.

halter
a rope with a head-piece for leading a horse.

halve
to divide into two equal parts.

ham
salted or smoked meat from a pig's leg.

hamburger
a cake of minced meat fried and eaten in a bread roll.

hammer
a tool with a metal head used to drive in nails.

hammock
a hanging mattress or bed held up by ropes.

hamper
1 a large basket with a lid.
2 to hinder.

hamster
a small animal like a large mouse, often kept as a pet.

hand
1 the part of the arm below the wrist.
2 a pointer on a clock.
3 to pass (something) to someone.

handbag
a bag carried in the hand.

handicap
something that keeps you back; a disadvantage.

handicapped
having something badly wrong with you (for example not being able to walk).

handkerchief
a small piece of cloth for wiping the nose.

handle
1 to touch with the hand.
2 the part of something which you hold in your hand.

handlebars
the part of a bicycle you hold on to to steer it.

handsome
good-looking.

handy
useful.

hang
to fasten something at the top so that it falls loose.

hanger
a piece of wood, plastic or wire specially shaped to hang clothes on.

happen	to take place, to occur.	**hatchet**	a small axe.
happy	feeling very pleased, glad.	**hate**	to dislike very much, to detest.
harass	to annoy, to cause difficulties.	**haul**	to drag, to pull with effort.
harbour	a place of shelter for boats.	**haunted**	often visited by a ghost.
hard	1 difficult to do. 2 tough, firm, not soft.	**have**	to possess, to own.
hardly	scarcely, only just.	**hawk**	a large bird which hunts small birds or animals for food.
hardy	strong, able to bear pain, for example; (of a plant) able to live in hard conditions.	**hay**	dried grass used as animal food.
hare	an animal like a large rabbit.	**haze**	very light mist or thin cloud.
harm	danger; trouble.	**hazel**	1 a small tree with brown nuts which you can eat. 2 a light-brown colour.
harness	the straps used to control a horse, for example.		
harp	a musical instrument which is played by plucking strings.	**head**	1 the part of the body above the neck. 2 the chief person. 3 the front part or top of something.
harpoon	a spear used in catching whales.		
harsh	rough, severe, unkind.	**headache**	a pain in the head.
harvest	1 a crop of food to be gathered in. 2 the time when this is done.	**heal**	to make well again after being hurt or ill, to cure.
haste	speed, quickness, hurry.	**health**	1 the state of your body or mind. 2 freedom from illness, fitness.
hat	a head covering, often with a brim.	**heap**	things placed one on top of another untidily, a pile.
hatch	1 to be born from an egg. 2 to make secret plans. 3 an opening in the deck of a ship, for example.	**hear**	1 to catch the sound of; to listen to. 2 to get news.

heart	1 the part of the body which pumps the blood round the body.
	2 the centre or most important part of something.
	3 a shape with two rounded parts at the top and a sharp point at the bottom.
	4 one of the four kinds in a pack of playing cards.
heat	1 warmth, being hot.
	2 one of the races leading to a final.
heather	a small plant with purple or white flowers which grows on moorlands.
heave	1 to pull strongly.
	2 to lift something and then throw it.
heaven	the place where God is said to live; perfect happiness.
heavy	having great weight, not easily lifted.
hedge	small bushes or trees grown in lines to separate fields or gardens.
hedgehog	a smallish animal with prickles on its back which rolls itself into a ball when in danger.
heel	the back part of the foot.
height	the distance from top to bottom, how tall something or someone is.
heir	a man or boy who receives a dead person's property.
heiress	a girl or woman who receives a dead person's property.
helicopter	an aeroplane which flies by means of a large overhead propeller.
hell	the place where the Devil is said to live; a place of very great suffering.
helmet	a covering to protect the head.
help	to do something for another person, to assist.
helpless	unable to do something for yourself, needing the help of others.
hem	an edge of cloth which has been turned over and stitched.
hemisphere	one of the two halves of the world.
hen	a female bird.
herb	a plant used for food, flavour and smell.
herd	a large number of the same kind of animals together.
hermit	a person who lives on his or her own, usually in a lonely place.
hero	1 a man or boy who acts with great bravery.
	2 the main man or boy in a story etc.
heroine	1 a woman or girl who acts with great bravery.
	2 the main woman or girl in a story etc.
herring	a sea-fish used for food.

hesitate	to stop what you are doing for a moment because you are not sure.
hibernate	to sleep through the winter as some animals do.
hiccup	a sudden noise in your throat, usually because you have eaten or drunk too quickly.
hide	1 to keep in a secret place. 2 to go where you cannot be found. 3 the skin of an animal.
hideous	terrible to look at, ugly, frightening.
high	1 tall, well above the ground. 2 great. 3 (of a sound) the opposite of low.
highwayman	(long ago) a man who stopped travellers and robbed them.
hill	a high piece of land often with steep sides.
hinder	something which makes it difficult for you to do something.
hinge	a moving joint which allows a door or window to open and close easily.
hint	to say something in a roundabout way; to suggest.
hip	the place where the legs join the body.
hippopotamus	a large African animal which lives near water.

hire	to borrow something for a short time and pay for its use.
hiss	to push air sharply through the teeth.
history	1 what happened in the past. 2 learning about the past.
hit	to strike, give a blow to or knock.
hive	where bees live.
hoarse	having a rough, harsh voice.
hobby	something you like doing in your spare time.
hockey	a game played by two teams with curved sticks and a ball.
hoe	a tool used for breaking up the soil and taking out weeds.
hold	1 to keep a grip of. 2 to have inside, to contain. 3 the storage part of a ship.
hole	an opening; a gap.
holiday	a time of rest and enjoyment; a time when you are free from work or school.
hollow	empty, with nothing inside.
holly	an evergreen bush with sharp, pointed leaves and red berries.

holy	connected with God or a god.
home	the place where you live.
honest	able to be trusted, truthful.
honey	a sweet food made by bees.
honour	1 great respect. 2 fame.
hood	1 a covering to protect the head and neck. 2 a folding cover for a baby's pram or for a motor car.
hoof	the hard part of the foot of some animals, for example horses.
hook	a bent and pointed piece of metal, plastic, etc. to hold or catch things.
hoop	a ring of wood, metal, etc.
hoot	1 the sound made by a car horn etc. 2 the sound made by an owl.
hop	to jump up and down on one foot.
hope	to wish and believe that something pleasant will happen.
hopeless	1 giving no reason for hope. 2 very bad.
horizon	the line where the sky and the earth seem to touch.

horn	1 a piece of hard material which grows out of the head of some animals. 2 a bell-shaped musical instrument you blow through. 3 a device on a car or bus which makes a noise to give a warning.
horrible	very unpleasant.
horrid	dreadful; causing fear.
horror	something very frightening or terrible.
horse	a large animal with hooves and a mane often used to ride on or to pull vehicles.
hose	a tube through which water can be directed.
hospital	a place where sick people are cared for.
hospitality	welcome shown to visitors or guests.
host	a man who invites others to his house as guests.
hostage	someone kept prisoner to force someone else to do something they don't want to do.
hostess	a woman who invites others to her house as guests.
hostile	very unfriendly.
hot	very warm.
hotel	a building where you can pay to stay the night or buy a meal.
hound	a dog which is trained to hunt.

hour — a length of time of 60 minutes.

house — a building in which people live.

hover — to stay in the air above a place or thing.

howl — a long, loud cry like that made by a wolf, for example; a wailing noise.

hub — the centre part of a wheel.

huff — a bad mood.

hug — to hold tightly in the arms.

huge — very large.

hum —
1 the noise like that made by bees.
2 to make the sound of a tune with the lips together.

human — connected with people.

humble — simple, modest, not proud.

humour —
1 finding or making things funny.
2 a mood.

hump — a large lump on the back of a person or an animal.

hundred — 100, a number.

hunger — a great need, usually for food.

hunt —
1 to try to catch or kill wild animals.
2 to look very carefully for something.

hurl — to throw far away.

hurricane — a storm with a very strong wind.

hurry — to move or do things very quickly; to rush.

hurt — to cause pain to, to injure, to damage.

husband — a married man.

hut — a small building, usually made of wood.

hyacinth — a sweet-smelling spring flower grown from a bulb.

hyena — an African or Asian animal like a large dog which hunts other animals and also feeds on dead bodies.

hymn — a religious song of praise or thanks.

I i

ice — frozen water.

iceberg — a very large piece of ice floating in the sea.

ice-cream — a soft, sweet, frozen food.

icicle — a hanging spike of ice.

icing — a sweet mixture sometimes spread over cakes and buns.

idea — a thought, something in the mind.

ideal — just what is needed, the best possible.

identical — exactly the same as something else.

idiot — a person who behaves stupidly.

idle	not working; not wanting to work.
igloo	a house made of snow blocks by Eskimos.
ignorant	not wise, knowing nothing or very little.
ignore	to pay no attention to, usually on purpose.
ill	not well; in poor health.
ill-treat	to treat badly.
illustrate	to explain something by drawing pictures; to add pictures to.
image	1 a figure carved in wood or stone, a statue. 2 a shadowy picture, a reflection.
imaginary	not real, made up in the mind.
imitate	to do the same as somebody else, to copy.
immediate	1 near, close. 2 taking place right away.
immediately	at once.
impertinent	rude, unmannerly, especially towards older people, cheeky.
impolite	rude, not polite.
import	to bring goods into a country from another country.
important	of great value, mattering very much.
impossible	not able to be done, not possible.

impress	to make (someone) notice and admire you.
imprison	to put into prison.
improve	to make (something) better; to get better.
incapable	not able to do something.
inch	a small measure of length equal to $\frac{1}{12}$ of a foot.
incident	a happening, something that takes place.
include	to put (something) in with other things.
income	money which is earned or received.
inconvenient	not suitable or helpful at a particular time.
incorrect	wrong.
increase	to make larger or greater.
indeed	as a matter of fact, really.
independent	able to act alone.
index	an alphabetical list showing where things can be found in a book.
indignant	angry, annoyed.
individual	a single person or thing.
infant	a baby; a young child.
infectious	(of an illness) likely to be passed on to someone else.
inflate	to put air into something causing it to swell.
inform	to tell; to give the news.
ingredient	one of a number of things which together make up something else, in cooking, for example.

inhabit	to live in (a certain place).	**insult**	to be rude to (someone) by saying unkind things about them.
initial	the first letter of a name.	**intelligent**	quick to learn, clever.
injection	the putting of medicine into the body with a special needle.	**intend**	to mean to do something.
		interest	keen attention.
injure	to hurt.	**interfere**	to get in the way of; to meddle.
ink	a coloured liquid used for writing or printing.	**interrupt**	to break into what other people are saying or doing.
inland	away from the sea.		
inn	a place where people can buy a drink or a meal, a small hotel.	**interval**	a break, a pause; a space between things.
innocent	not guilty; not at fault.	**interview**	a meeting at which people ask and answer questions.
inquire	to ask questions.		
insane	not in your right mind, mad.	**introduce**	to make people known to each other.
insect	a small flying or crawling creature with six legs.	**invade**	to enter, usually using force.
inside	the part which is surrounded by something else; the part within.	**invent**	to think of and make something for the first time.
insist	to keep on saying something.	**invisible**	not able to be seen.
inspect	to look carefully at (something).	**invitation**	asking someone to your house or to go out with you.
instant	1 a moment. 2 made in a moment (for example **instant coffee**).	**invite**	to ask somebody to come to your house, or to go out with you.
instead of	in place of.	**iron**	1 a hard, strong metal. 2 a tool for pressing clothes.
instruct	to teach someone how to do something.		
instrument	1 a tool. 2 something which is made to give out musical sounds.	**irritate**	1 to make annoyed or angry. 2 to make sore.
		island	a piece of land with water all round it.

itch — a tickling of the skin that makes you want to scratch.

item — one thing out of a number of things.

ivory — the hard, white material elephants' tusks are made from.

ivy — a climbing, evergreen plant.

J j

jab — to poke at or to stab with something pointed.

jackal — a wild animal that looks like a dog.

jacket — a short coat.

jail — a prison. The word may also be spelt **gaol**.

jam
1 a food made from boiled fruit and sugar.
2 to become fixed or difficult to move.
3 a crowding together (for example of traffic).

jar
1 a container with an opening at the top.
2 a movement or sound that makes you shudder.

jaw — the bones to which teeth are fixed; the lower part of the face.

jazz — a kind of modern music.

jealous — annoyed because you wish you had what others have, envious.

jeans — trousers made from strong, usually blue, cotton.

jeep — a small, powerful motor car.

jeer — to make rude remarks about something.

jelly — a soft, clear food made from fruit juice.

jerk — a sudden push or pull.

jersey — a piece of knitted clothing for the upper part of the body.

jet
1 a thin stream of water or air.
2 an engine driven by a stream of air passing through special tubes.

jewel — a valuable stone often used for ornament.

jewellery — ornaments that you wear made of precious stones or metal or imitations of these.

jigsaw (puzzle) — a kind of puzzle in which many little pieces are put together to make a picture.

jingle — to make a ringing sound with small metal objects.

job
1 a piece of work.
2 the work you do for a living.

jockey — the rider of a racehorse.

jog
1 to run at a slow, steady pace.
2 to push lightly.

join
1 to fasten together.
2 to become a member of a club etc.

joiner   a person who works with wood, a carpenter.

joint
1 the place where two parts fit together.
2 a large piece of meat.

joke   something you say to make people laugh.

jolly   merry, happy, lively.

jolt   a sudden jerk.

journey   a trip from place to place.

joy   happiness, gladness.

judge
1 the person in court who has the final say in matters of law.
2 someone who decides the result of a competition.
3 to decide the value of something.

judo   a kind of Japanese fighting, now often used as a sport.

jug   a container for pouring liquids.

juggler   a person who can keep several objects in the air at the same time without dropping them.

juice   the liquid which comes from fruit and vegetables.

jumble   a muddle; many things mixed together in an untidy way.

jump   to spring into the air with both feet off the ground.

jumper   a knitted garment worn on the top part of the body.

junction   a place where two or more railway lines or roads meet or cross.

jungle   a thick forest in very hot countries.

junior   younger or lower in importance than others.

junk
1 rubbish that is of no use to anyone.
2 a kind of Chinese sailing-boat.

just
1 fair; right.
2 only.

jut   to stick out.

K k

kangaroo   an Australian animal with long back legs on which it jumps.

karate   a kind of Japanese fighting, now often used as a sport.

keel   the bottom part of a boat on which the rest of the boat is built.

keen
1 anxious to do what should be done, eager.
2 sharp.

keep   to hold; to have for oneself.

kennel   a small house for a dog.

kerb   the border or edge of a pavement.

kernel   the centre part of a nut, the part you eat.

kettle	a container with a handle and spout, used to boil water.
key	1 a tool to open or close a lock.
	2 a part of a musical instrument or a typewriter that you press down.
kick	to hit with the foot.
kid	1 a young goat.
	2 the leather made from a goat's skin.
kidnap	to seize (a person) and keep them until money is paid for their safe return.
kidney	1 one of two small parts of the inside of the body.
	2 the kidney of an animal used as food.
kill	to put to death, to cause to die.
kilogram	a measure of weight equal to a thousand grams.
kilometre	a measure of length equal to a thousand metres.
kilt	a pleated skirt, usually of tartan cloth, sometimes worn by men in Scotland.
kind	1 a type, a sort.
	2 good, helpful, gentle.
king	a male ruler of a country.
kingdom	an area ruled over by a king or queen.
kipper	a herring split open and smoked.

kiss	to touch with the lips.
kit	things you need in order to do something.
kitchen	a room used for cooking.
kite	a light frame covered with cloth or paper for flying at the end of a long string.
kitten	a young cat.
knee	the joint in the middle of the leg.
kneel	to place one or both knees on the ground.
knickers	underpants worn by women and girls.
knife	a sharp blade with a handle used for cutting.
knight	1 a title given to a man by a king or queen; then 'Sir' is put in front of his name.
	2 (long ago) a man who fought battles on horseback.
knit	to join loops of wool etc. using long needles or machines.
knob	a round handle used on doors and furniture.
knock	1 to make a tapping noise (for example at a door).
	2 to strike hard.
knot	a fastening made by twisting string or rope.
know	1 to have something in your mind.
	2 to recognize (someone).

knowledge something you know and understand.

knuckle a joint of a finger.

L l

label a paper or card for fastening on to a parcel etc.

labour hard work.

lace
1 an open-work pattern made from fine thread.
2 a strong string to tie a shoe.

lack to be without something.

lad a boy.

ladder a frame with bars for getting up to high places.

ladle a large, deep spoon with a long handle, used for serving soup etc.

lady
1 a polite name for a woman.
2 a title given to a woman, sometimes because of her husband's or father's title.

ladybird a small beetle, often red with black spots.

lag to move slowly, to fall behind others.

lair a wild animal's den.

lake a large stretch of water with land all round it.

lamb a young sheep.

lame not able to walk properly, limping.

lamp something made for giving light.

lance a long, thin spear.

land
1 the part of the earth not covered by the sea.
2 to come to land from air or water.
3 a country.

lane a narrow road.

language the words used by the people of a particular country.

lantern a case in which a light is carried.

lap
1 the space formed on the top of your thighs when you are sitting down.
2 to drink using the tongue, like a dog or cat.
3 once round a racetrack.

larch a kind of tree with cones which loses its leaves in winter.

large big, huge.

lark a small singing bird.

lash
1 to fasten tightly with rope or string.
2 to whip, to hit hard.
3 a small hair on the eyelid.

lasso
(say 'las<u>soo</u>') a rope with a noose at the end for catching animals.

last	*1* coming after all the others. *2* to go on for a period of time.
late	*1* behind time. *2* near the end of a period of time.
lather	*1* bubbles made in water when using soap. *2* sweat produced by a horse when working hard.
laugh	the sound you make when you are amused or happy.
launch	*1* a motor boat. *2* to float a newly-built boat.
launderette	a place where you can wash and dry clothes by putting money into the machines there.
laundry	*1* a place where clothing is taken to be washed. *2* a pile of clothing ready for washing or ironing.
lavatory	a toilet.
law	a rule made by the government that everyone must obey.
lawn	an area of short grass in a garden or in a park.
lawyer	a person who has studied the law and can advise people about it.
lay	*1* to put down. *2* to produce eggs.
lazy	not fond of working, liking to do nothing.

lead (rhymes with 'bed')	a heavy metal.
lead (rhymes with 'feed')	*1* to go in front for others to follow. *2* a strap or chain fixed to a dog's collar in order to control the animal.
leader	the person in charge of a group, the head person.
leaf	*1* one of the flat, green parts of a tree or other plant. *2* a page of a book.
league	a group of sporting teams who play games against each other to find a winner.
leak	a hole or gap from which liquid or gas can escape.
lean	*1* to bend towards something. *2* thin, not fat. *3* **lean against** to put your weight against (something).
leap	to jump, to spring.
learn	to get to know; to become good at doing something.
least	the smallest amount.
leather	an animal's skin which has been prepared for making into shoes or handbags, for example.
leave	*1* to go away from. *2* to let (something) stay where it is.

lecture   a speech made to a number of people usually to teach something.

ledge   a narrow shelf.

leek   a long, white and green vegetable which tastes rather like an onion.

left   the same side of the body as the heart, the opposite of right.

leg   1 one of the limbs with which you walk.
2 one of the supports at the corner of a table, for example.

legal   to do with the law.

legend   a story from long ago, which may not be true.

leisure   spare time used for hobbies and enjoying yourself.

lemon   a yellow fruit with a sharp taste.

lemonade   a sweet, fizzy drink flavoured with lemon.

lend   to allow somebody to use (something) for a time.

length   the distance from one end to the other.

leopard   a large wild animal of the cat family with spotted fur.

leotard   a close-fitting, single garment worn for gymnastics, dancing, etc.

less   smaller, not so big, not so much.

lesson   something to be learned.

let   1 to allow, to permit.
2 to allow someone to use (a building) in return for a rent.

letter   1 a written message sent to somebody.
2 one of the signs we use for writing, such as a, b, c.

lettuce   a broad-leaved, green vegetable used in salads.

level   1 the same height all along, flat.
2 equal.

lever   a strong metal bar for lifting things.

liar   a person who tells lies.

librarian   a person who works in a library.

library   a room or building where books are stored.

licence   a printed paper that gives you permission to do something.

lick   to wet or rub with the tongue.

lid   a cover that can be opened or taken off.

lie   1 to rest in a flat position.
2 to say things that are not true.
3 something which is not true.

life   the time when you are alive.

lifeboat   a boat kept ready to go to the help of people in danger on the sea.

lift
1 to raise.
2 a machine which carries people or goods up and down in a building.
3 a ride in someone's car etc.

light
1 brightness, the opposite of darkness.
2 pale in colour, not dark.
3 having little weight, easy to lift.
4 to make something burn (for example a fire or a lamp).

lighthouse
a tall building or tower with a powerful light on top to warn ships of danger.

lightning
a flash of light you see in the sky during a thunderstorm.

like
1 to be fond of.
2 the same as, similar to.

likely
what you would expect.

lilac
1 a small tree with sweet-smelling purple or white flowers.
2 a pale-purple colour, like these flowers.

lily
a beautiful flower, often white in colour.

limb
an arm, a leg or a wing.

lime
1 a greenish fruit like a small lemon.
2 a kind of tree with large pale-green leaves.
3 a white powder made from limestone.

limestone
a greyish-white rock.

limit
the end, as far as you can go.

limp
1 to walk as if one foot or leg has been hurt.
2 not firm or stiff.

line
1 a long, thin mark.
2 a piece of rope or string.
3 people or things standing one behind the other.

linen
a kind of thin cloth used for making sheets or tablecloths, for example.

liner
a large passenger ship.

lining
cloth used on the inside of clothes.

link
one of the rings in a chain.

lion
a large wild animal of the cat family, found mainly in Africa.

lip
one of the soft, round edges of the mouth.

lipstick
colouring for the lips.

liquid
something which flows (for example water or milk).

liquorice
a kind of chewy, black sweet made from a plant root.

list
a number of names or things written down one after the other.

listen
1 to try to hear.
2 to take notice of what someone is saying.

literature
well-written stories and poems.

litre — a measure of liquid.

litter —
1 rubbish lying about.
2 a number of animals born together.

little — small, tiny, not big.

live —
1 to stay in a place.
2 to be alive.

lively — full of life, active.

liver —
1 a part of the inside of the body.
2 the liver of an animal used as food.

lizard — an animal with four short legs, a long tail and skin like a snake.

load —
1 as much as can be carried at one time.
2 to put goods on to (a ship or vehicle).
3 to put bullets into (a gun).

loaf — a large piece of bread which you cut in slices.

loan — something that is lent or borrowed.

lobster — a kind of large shellfish with claws.

local — near a particular place, near where you are.

loch — a Scottish lake.

lock —
1 to fasten something so that only a key will open it.
2 a place in a canal or river where boats are raised or lowered.
3 a piece of hair.

locust — an insect like a grasshopper which destroys crops.

loft — the space under the roof of a building.

log —
1 a part of a tree sawn off for building or for firewood.
2 a ship's diary.

lonely —
1 feeling sad and alone; without friends.
2 (of a house etc.) with no others near it.

long —
1 of great length, not short.
2 to wish for something very much.

look —
1 to try to see.
2 to appear to be, to seem.

loom —
1 a machine for weaving.
2 to come into sight slowly, often out of mist or darkness.

loop — a shape like a ring made in string or rope, for example.

loose — not tied or fixed, free to move, slack.

lord — a title given to a man by a king or queen.

lorry — a large motor vehicle for carrying heavy loads.

lose —
1 not to be able to find (something), to stop having.
2 to be beaten, not to win.

loss — something you have lost.

lotion	a liquid for putting on the skin to improve or protect it.
loud	making a lot of noise, easily heard.
lounge	1 a sitting-room. 2 to act lazily.
love	to like very much.
lovely	beautiful.
low	1 not high, near to the ground or the bottom of something. 2 quiet, not loud.
loyal	able to be trusted to defend friends or country.
luck	fortune, chance.
lucky	having good luck.
luggage	bags and suitcases you take with you when travelling.
lukewarm	neither very hot nor very cold.
lullaby	a quiet song to send a baby to sleep.
lump	1 a swelling. 2 a piece of something.
lunatic	a mad person.
lunch	a meal eaten in the middle of the day.
lung	one of the two parts of the body with which you breathe.
lurk	to wait in hiding, especially for a bad purpose.
luxury	something expensive you like having but do not need.

M m

machine	something made out of many parts that work together to do a job.
machinery	machines; parts of a machine.
mackerel	a kind of sea-fish used as food.
mackintosh	a raincoat, a waterproof.
mad	1 insane, crazy; very foolish. 2 very angry.
madam	a polite way of speaking or writing to a woman.
magazine	a paper containing stories, pictures, etc. sold every week or month.
maggot	a grub which turns into a fly, sometimes found in bad meat, for example.
magic	1 strange and wonderful things which happen by a strange power. 2 clever or strange tricks done to amuse.
magician	a person who performs magic tricks.
magnet	a piece of iron or steel which attracts other pieces of iron or steel.
magnificent	splendid.
magnify	to make (something) appear larger.
magpie	a black and white bird with a long tail which likes to pick up brightly-coloured objects.

maid	1 a woman servant. 2 an old-fashioned word for a girl.
mail	1 letters and parcels sent by post. 2 (long ago) a kind of armour worn by soldiers.
main	most important, chief.
maize	a kind of grain used for food, sweet corn.
Majesty	a title given to a king or queen.
major	1 an officer in the army. 2 the chief, the most important.
make	1 to build; to create. 2 to force (somebody) to do something.
male	a person or an animal that can become a father; a man or boy.
mammal	an animal which feeds its young with its own milk.
mammoth	1 a kind of large elephant of long ago. 2 very big, huge.
man	a grown-up male person.
manage	1 to be able to do something. 2 to take charge of something.
mane	the long hair on the neck of an animal, especially a horse or lion.
manger	an animal's feeding-box in a stable.
mankind	the human race.

manner	1 the way in which we behave. 2 the way in which a thing is done.
manners	behaviour, especially good behaviour towards other people.
mansion	a very large house.
manufacture	to make things in a factory by using machinery.
many	a large number of, plenty.
map	a drawing of a large surface, showing its main features (for example rivers, mountains, roads).
maple	a kind of tree which produces a syrup.
marble	1 a hard stone which can be smoothly polished. 2 a small, round glass or stone ball with which children play.
march	1 to walk in step with others. 2 a piece of music to which people, especially soldiers, march.
mare	a female horse.
margarine	a food made from vegetable oils which is often used instead of butter.
margin	a border down the side of a page.
mark	1 a sign put on something. 2 a spot, a stain. 3 the number you reach in a test. 4 to put a mark on.

market   a place, often in the open air, where goods are bought and sold.

marmalade   a kind of jam made of oranges, lemons, etc.

maroon
1 a very dark red colour.
2 to leave (someone) somewhere where they cannot get away (for example on an island).

marriage   a wedding.

marry   to become someone's husband or wife.

marsh   wet land, a swamp, a bog.

marvellous   wonderful.

marzipan   a paste made from almonds, egg and sugar, put on cakes.

mascot   a charm, a thing or an animal supposed to bring good luck.

masculine   concerning men or boys.

mash   to crush to a soft, smooth state (for example potatoes).

mask   a covering for the face.

mass
1 a large amount of something.
2 a crowd of people.
3 a religious ceremony, especially in a Roman Catholic church.

massive   very large, enormous.

mast   the tall pole used to hold up the sails on a ship.

master   the chief man, the man in charge.

mat
1 a small rug.
2 a small piece of material for putting under dishes.

match
1 a small, thin stick with a tip which catches fire when rubbed.
2 a game between two teams.
3 to be the same as (something else).

mate   companion.

material
1 anything from which things can be made.
2 cloth.

mathematics   the study of numbers, shapes and measurements.

matter
1 to be important.
2 something you think about.

mattress   a large, thick layer of material on which you sleep.

maybe   perhaps, possibly.

mayor   the chief person in a town.

maze   a lot of paths and lines arranged so that it is difficult to find your way through them.

meadow   an area of grassland.

meal
1 the food you eat at a certain time of day.
2 grain ground into a kind of flour.

mean
1 not generous.
2 to have a meaning.
3 **mean to** to have it in your mind to.

meaning — what you have in your mind when you say or write something, an explanation.

measles — an illness which gives you red spots.

measure — 1 to find out how long, broad, heavy, etc. something is.
2 a unit for measuring.

measurement — what something measures.

meat — flesh from an animal used as food.

mechanic — a person who makes or repairs machinery.

medal — a disc of metal etc. given as a reward for something you have done.

meddle — to interfere with things which are not your business.

medicine — something you take to make you better when you are ill.

medium — not big or small, in between.

meek — gentle, humble.

meet — 1 to come together.
2 to go to see and greet (someone).

melody — a tune.

melon — a large, juicy fruit with a green or yellow skin.

melt — to become liquid because of heat.

member — a person who belongs to a group.

memory — 1 the part of the brain with which you remember.
2 a thought about the past.

mend — to put right, to repair.

mental — to do with the mind.

mention — to talk about.

menu — a list of things you can eat in a restaurant.

merchant — a person who buys and sells.

mercy — pity, not punishing someone.

merry — happy, cheerful, joyful.

mess — things mixed together in an untidy, dirty way.

message — news sent from one person to another.

metal — materials such as iron, steel, gold, silver and brass.

meteor — a small object from space which travels very fast and burns out when it enters the earth's atmosphere.

meter — a machine for measuring such things as gas or electricity.

method — the way in which something is done.

metre — a measure of length equal to one hundred centimetres.

microcomputer — a small computer you can use at home or at school.

microphone	an instrument which picks up sounds and makes them louder.
microscope	an instrument used to make very small things look much bigger.
midday	twelve o'clock in the day.
middle	the part of something that is the same distance from all of its sides or its ends.
midnight	twelve o'clock at night.
mild	1 gentle, not rough. 2 not too hot or too cold.
mile	a measure of length equal to 1760 yards.
milk	a white liquid given by mothers and some female animals to feed their babies.
mill	1 a place where grain is ground into flour or meal. 2 a factory, especially one where cloth is made.
millimetre	a measure of length equal to a thousandth of a metre.
million	1 000 000, a number.
millionaire	a very rich person who has at least a million pounds.
mime	to use actions instead of words to show the meaning of something.
mimic	to speak or act like someone else.

mince	1 to cut up into very small pieces. 2 meat cut up in this way.
mind	1 a person's way of thinking; the power to think. 2 to look after. 3 to object to (something).
mine	1 belonging to me. 2 a place where coal, salt, etc. are dug from the earth.
mineral	things such as rock which are dug out of the earth.
mingle	to mix.
miniature	very small, but like something bigger.
minister	1 a person in charge of a church, a clergyman. 2 an important member of a government.
minor	1 smaller or less important. 2 the younger one.
mint	1 a plant used to flavour food. 2 a sweet flavoured with mint. 3 a place where coins are made.
minus	less than, without; the sign — .
minute (say 'minit')	a length of time of sixty seconds.
minute (say 'my<u>newt</u>')	very small.

miracle	a strange and wonderful happening which is thought to be the work of God.
mirror	a piece of glass in which you can see yourself.
mischief	stupid actions which cause trouble.
mischievous	always doing mischief.
miser	a person who has plenty of money, but tries not to spend any.
miserable	full of sadness.
misery	great unhappiness, sorrow.
miss	1 not to see or find; not to succeed. 2 **Miss** a title given to an unmarried woman or girl.
mission	an important task that someone is sent to do.
missionary	a person who is sent to other places to teach people about religion.
mist	drops of water in the air which stop you from seeing properly, fog.
mistake	something you have done or thought which is wrong, an error.
mistletoe	an evergreen plant with white berries, often used as a Christmas decoration.
mistress	the chief woman, the woman in charge.
mitten	a glove with only two parts, one for the fingers and one for the thumb.
mix	to put things together (for example by stirring or shaking).
mixture	things mixed together.
moan	a low sound made when you are in pain or unhappy.
moat	a ditch round a castle to keep it safe from attack.
mock	to make fun of (someone), especially by doing the same as they do.
model	1 a copy of something. 2 a pattern to be followed. 3 a person whose job is to wear clothes in order to display them, for example for a photograph.
modern	up-to-date, belonging to the present time.
moist	a little wet, damp.
mole	1 a small, furry animal which burrows underground. 2 a small, dark spot on the skin.
moment	a very short space of time.
monarch	a ruler of a country who is a king or queen.
monastery	a place where monks live.
money	the coins and pieces of paper you use for buying and selling.
mongrel	a dog of two or more breeds.

monk	a man who has given his life to his religion and who lives in a monastery.
monkey	an animal with a long tail and with hands and feet like a person. It lives in trees in hot countries.
monster	a large, frightening animal, especially an imaginary one.
month	1 one of the twelve parts of the year (for example August). 2 a period of four weeks.
monument	something built in memory of an important person or event.
mood	the way you feel.
moon	the planet that goes round the earth and is sometimes seen shining in the sky.
moor	1 a large area of rough ground, covered with grass and heather. 2 to fasten a boat with a rope.
mop	soft material at the end of long pole, used for cleaning.
moral	a lesson about right and wrong (for example one you learn from a story).
more	a greater number or amount.
morning	the part of the day before noon.
mosque	a place where Muslims worship.
mosquito	a small flying insect that bites and can pass on disease.
moss	a furry, green plant which grows on wet stones and trees.
most	the greatest number or amount.
moth	an insect like a butterfly which usually flies at night.
mother	a female parent.
motion	movement.
motor	an engine to make things move or turn.
mould	1 to make (something) into a new shape. 2 a container for shaping things.
mound	a large heap; a small hill.
mount	to get onto (a horse or a bicycle, for example).
mountain	a very high hill.
mourn	to be very sad for the death of someone or for the loss of something.
mouse	a very small animal with a long tail.
moustache	hair growing on the upper lip.
mouth	1 the part of the head with which you speak, eat and drink. 2 where a river goes into the sea.
move	to go or take from one place to another.
mow	to cut grass.

Mr.
(say 'mister')
title given to a man.

Mrs.
(say 'missiz')
title given to a married woman.

much   a large quantity.

mud   wet earth.

muddle   a mixed-up state.

mug   a big cup with straight sides.

mule   an animal whose parents were a horse and a donkey.

multiply   to increase something a number of times.

mumble   to speak in a way that is difficult to hear and understand.

mummy
1 a dead body that has been preserved.
2 **Mummy** a name for your mother.

mumps   a painful illness of the neck.

munch   to eat noisily.

murder   to kill (someone) on purpose.

murmur   to speak very quietly.

muscle   one of the parts of the body that help you to move.

museum   a building where old and interesting things can be seen.

mushroom   a plant shaped like a small umbrella, used as food.

music   pleasant sounds made by voices singing or by instruments.

musical
1 to do with music.
2 a special type of film or a play using music.

mussel   a kind of shellfish used as food.

mustard   a hot-tasting, yellow powder or paste used to flavour food.

mutter   to speak or complain in a low voice.

mutton   meat from sheep.

muzzle
1 an animal's mouth and nose.
2 a covering put over an animal's mouth.
3 the open end of a gun barrel.

mysterious   very strange.

mystery   something strange which cannot be explained.

N n

nag   to keep finding fault with (someone).

nail
1 a small, sharp-pointed piece of metal used to join pieces of wood together.
2 the hard, shiny covering at the end of a finger or toe.

naked   not wearing any clothes, not covered, bare.

name	what you call someone or something, the word you use when talking about a person or thing.
napkin	a small piece of cloth or paper used at the table to keep your clothes clean while you eat.
nappy	a piece of cloth or paper wrapped round a baby's bottom.
narrow	not far across, not wide.
nasty	not pleasant; not good to taste; not kind.
nation	the people of one country.
national	belonging to a nation.
native	a person born in a certain place.
natural	made by nature, not man-made.
nature	1 everything in the world not man-made (for example animals, plants, rocks). 2 the way people or other living things behave.
naughty	badly behaved.
naval	to do with a navy.
navigate	to tell which way a ship, an aeroplane or a car should go.
navy	1 a country's warships and sailors. 2 a dark blue colour.
near	close to; not far away.
nearly	almost, not quite.

neat	tidy and clean.
necessary	something you must have or that must be done.
neck	the part of the body joining the head and shoulders.
necklace	a string of beads or jewels worn round the neck.
need	1 to want badly. 2 **need to** to have to.
needle	a thin, sharp piece of metal with a hole at one end, used for sewing.
negative	a piece of film from which you can make a photograph.
neglect	not to do something that should be done; not to look after.
neigh	the sound a horse makes.
neighbour	a person who lives next door or quite near.
nephew	a son of a brother or sister.
nerve	one of the small parts of the body which carry messages to and from the brain.
nervous	afraid; easily frightened or worried.
nest	a place used as a home by birds and some animals.
net	material made of string or wire with open spaces which catch solid objects but let air or liquid through the holes.

netball	a team game in which a ball is thrown into a high net.
nettle	a wild plant which can sting when touched.
new	just made or bought; not used or known before.
news	telling or writing about something that has happened.
newspaper	folded sheets of paper giving news etc. printed every day or every week.
newt	a land or water animal like a small lizard.
next	1 nearest, with nothing between. 2 following.
nibble	to eat in tiny bites.
nice	pleasant.
nickname	a name that is not your real name.
niece	a daughter of a brother or sister.
night	the time of darkness.
nightmare	a bad or frightening dream.
nimble	quick and light on your feet.
nine	9, a number.
nineteen	19, a number.
ninety	90, a number.
nip	to bite, to pinch.
noble	1 of very good character. 2 of high rank in society.
nobleman	a man of high rank.
nod	to bend your head forward quickly, often as a sign that you mean 'yes'.
noise	a sound, often loud and unpleasant.
none	not any, not one.
nonsense	words that have no sense or meaning, foolishness.
noon	twelve o'clock midday.
noose	a loop in a rope which can be made tighter by pulling.
normal	usual, the same as others.
north	the direction that is on the left as you face the rising sun.
nose	the part of your face with which you breathe and smell things.
nostril	one of the two openings in your nose.
notch	a small v-shaped cut.
note	1 a short letter. 2 a single sound in music. 3 a piece of paper money.
notice	1 to see something. 2 a piece of paper, often pinned to a wall, which tells you something.
noun	a word which tells you what a person or thing is called.

now	at this moment, at this time.
nozzle	the open end of a tube or spout.
nude	not wearing any clothes.
nudge	a slight push.
nugget	a rough lump found in the earth, containing metal, especially gold.
nuisance	something which annoys you or holds you up.
numb	not having any feeling.
number	1 a word or figure, such as one, two, three, 1, 2, 3, which tells you how many. 2 more than one person or thing.
numerous	many.
nun	a woman who has given her life to religion and lives in a convent.
nurse	a person trained to look after sick people or young children.
nursery	1 a room or building for young children. 2 a place where young plants are grown.
nut	1 the seed of a tree. 2 a piece of metal which screws onto a bolt.
nutmeg	a spice used in cooking.
nylon	a kind of strong cloth made from artificial threads.

O o

oak	a large tree with hard wood.
oar	a long piece of wood, flat at one end, used to push a boat through the water.
oasis	a place in the desert where water can be found and some plants grow.
oats	a plant which produces grain used for food (for example porridge).
obedience	when you obey.
obey	to do as you are told.
object	something that you can see or touch.
object	to say that you do not like or agree to something.
oblige	1 to do someone a favour. 2 to force (someone) to do something.
oblong	a shape which is longer than it is broad, like this page.
observe	to see, to look at, to notice.
obstacle	something which is in the way.
obstinate	not willing to change your mind or give way to others.
obstruct	to block the way, to hold back.
obtain	to get.

obvious	easy to see or understand.
occasion	a time when something happens.
occasionally	sometimes, not very often.
occupation	your job, what you work at.
occupy	1 to live in. 2 to take up space or time.
occur	1 to take place, to happen. 2 to come into your mind.
ocean	a very large sea.
o'clock	the hour shown by the clock.
octopus	a large sea creature with eight arms.
odd	1 not even: 1, 3, 5, etc. are **odd** numbers. 2 strange, unusual.
off	1 away from. 2 not on.
offend	to hurt someone's feelings.
offer	1 to say that you are ready to do something. 2 to hold (something) out for someone to take.
office	a place where people do business.
officer	1 a person who is in charge of other people (for example in the army). 2 a person with an important position in an organisation.

often	many times.
ogre	(in stories) a giant who eats people.
oil	a greasy liquid.
ointment	a healing cream put on cuts and bruises.
old	1 of great age, not new or young. 2 having lived for a certain number of years.
omelette	eggs beaten together and fried in butter.
once	1 one time. 2 in the past.
one	1 1, a number. 2 a single person or thing.
onion	a vegetable with a strong smell, made up of a lot of skins.
only	1 by itself, singly. 2 not more than.
onward	on and on, forward.
ooze	to flow slowly.
open	not shut, not covered over.
operate	1 to work (a machine). 2 to cut the body open to make it healthy again.
opinion	what you think about something.
opponent	someone who disagrees with you or fights against you.
opportunity	the chance or the time to do something.

opposite	1 on the other side of a place or an argument. 2 the side facing you. 3 as different as possible.
optician	a person who fits you with glasses or contact lenses to improve your eyesight.
orange	1 a juicy, reddish-yellow fruit grown in some hot countries. 2 the colour of this fruit.
orbit	the path of one body round another in space.
orchard	a place where fruit trees are grown.
orchestra	a large group of musicians playing together.
ordeal	a time when you suffer a lot of pain, fear or worry.
order	1 neatly arranged things or ideas. 2 to say what must be done.
ordinary	usual, what you expect.
ore	rock in which metal is found.
organ	1 a large musical instrument with many pipes, played like a piano. 2 a part of the inside of the body.
original	the earliest, the first one.
ornament	something used for decoration, especially in a room.
orphan	a child whose father and mother have both died.

ostrich	a very large African bird which cannot fly.
other	not the same, different.
otter	a fish-eating animal which lives near water.
ounce	a measure of weight, equal to a sixteenth of a pound.
out	1 not inside. 2 not lit.
outfit	a complete set of clothes or equipment.
outing	a journey made for pleasure, a trip.
outlaw	(long ago) a person who continually broke the law.
outline	the outside edge or shape of something or someone.
outside	1 the part of something that is on the surface. 2 not inside.
outskirts	the parts of a town which are not in the centre.
outwards	moving away from the centre of something.
oval	egg-shaped.
oven	a heated box for cooking and baking.
over	1 above. 2 done, finished. 3 more than. 4 across.
overalls	a special piece of clothing for working in, worn over your ordinary clothes.
overboard	over the side of a ship.

overcoat — a long coat worn over your clothes to keep you warm and dry.

overhead — above you, in the sky.

overlook — 1 to take no notice of.
2 to look down on.

overtake — to catch up with and then pass.

owe — to be in debt; to have to pay.

owl — a large bird which hunts at night.

own — 1 belonging to yourself.
2 to have, to possess.

ox — a kind of bull which is usually kept to pull heavy loads and ploughs.

oxygen — a gas without taste, smell or colour which is an important part of air and water and is necessary to keep you alive.

oyster — a kind of shellfish used for food.

P p

pace — 1 a step, a stride.
2 the speed at which you walk, run or move.

pack — 1 to put into a box, parcel or suitcase.
2 a group of things such as playing-cards.
3 a group of animals that hunt together.

packet — a small box or container made of paper or cardboard.

pad — 1 several sheets of paper stuck together at the top edge.
2 a piece of soft material such as cotton wool.
3 the thick skin on the feet of some animals.

paddle — 1 a piece of wood with a broad, flat end for driving a canoe or small boat.
2 to walk in shallow water.

padlock — a small lock on a ring which is not fixed to the thing it is locking.

page — a leaf of a book or newspaper.

pageant — a colourful parade or display of scenes from history.

pail — a bucket.

pain — a feeling of being hurt or suffering.

paint — a coloured liquid put on with a brush etc. to colour something.

painting — a picture which is painted.

pair — two things of the same kind or which always go together, such as socks or gloves.

palace — a large building often lived in by kings and queens.

pale — with little colour.

palm — 1 a kind of tree which grows in hot countries.
2 the flat front of the hand.

pamper	to be over-kind to.
pan	a round metal pot with a long handle, used for cooking.
pancake	a thin cake of flour, eggs, milk and sugar which is fried in a pan.
panda	a black and white animal like a small bear found in China.
pane	a piece of glass for a window.
panel	a piece of wood or other material fitted into a frame or into a door.
panic	sudden alarm or fear which makes a person or people behave in a stupid or thoughtless way.
pant	to breathe quickly as though you are short of breath.
panther	a large, black wild animal of the cat family.
pantomime	a fairy story performed on the stage with music and songs.
pants	1 underpants. 2 trousers.
paper	1 material for writing on, making books, wrapping things and so on. 2 a newspaper.
parable	a story, usually from the Bible, which has a special meaning.
parachute	cloth shaped like an umbrella, used when jumping from aircraft.
parade	1 a marching display by people in uniform. 2 to march up and down.
paradise	a place of complete happiness, heaven.
paraffin	thin oil used in lamps and stoves.
paragraph	a group of sentences.
paralysed	unable to move some or all of the body (for example because of serious injury).
parcel	something wrapped up for posting or carrying.
pardon	forgiveness for something you have done wrong.
parent	a father or mother.
parish	a district looked after by a clergyman.
park	1 a piece of land usually with grass and flowers where you can go to play or enjoy yourself. 2 a games field. 3 to leave (a car) somewhere for a time.
parliament	1 a group of people who make the laws of a country. 2 the place where they meet.
parrot	a bird which can learn to talk and which has bright feathers.
parsley	a herb used in cooking.
parsnip	a pale root vegetable.
parson	a minister, a clergyman.

part	1 a piece or portion of a whole thing.
	2 a share in some activity.
	3 to split up, to separate.
particular	1 special, different from others.
	2 hard to please.
partner	1 one of two people playing a game or dancing together, for example.
	2 a person sharing in a business.
party	a group of people gathered together, usually to enjoy themselves.
pass	1 to leave behind, to go past.
	2 to get through (a test).
	3 a gap in the mountains.
	4 a piece of paper that lets you get into places.
passage	1 a narrow way through.
	2 a piece taken from a book or story.
passenger	a person who travels by train, bus, ship, aeroplane, etc.
passport	an official document which allows you to travel abroad.
past	1 the time that has gone before.
	2 up to and away from.
paste	a wet and sticky mixture.
pastime	a hobby, interesting work done in your spare time.
pastry	the crispy baked casing of pies, tarts, etc.

pat	to touch gently with the hand.
patch	a small piece of material used to repair a hole (for example in clothes).
path	a narrow track for walking.
patient	1 taking something calmly, able to wait for things to be right.
	2 someone who is ill and seeing a doctor, dentist, etc.
patrol	a small group of policemen or soldiers (for example on the lookout for something).
patter	the sound made by:
	1 raindrops.
	2 running feet.
pattern	1 a design, a careful placing together of shapes and colours.
	2 a plan to follow when making something.
pause	a short stop or wait.
pavement	the part at each side of the street you walk on.
paw	a foot of an animal such as a dog or cat.
pay	1 to hand over money for something.
	2 money you are given for working.
pea	a seed which grows in a pod, used as food.
peace	1 quietness, stillness, calm.
	2 not being at war.

peach	a soft, juicy fruit with a yellowish-red skin and a large, hard seed called a stone inside.	**peer**	1 to look at closely. 2 a person of high rank.
peacock	a large male bird which makes its tail go into a huge, brightly-coloured fan-shape.	**peg**	1 a small hook for hanging clothes. 2 a small clip for fixing clothes to a washing-line.
peak	1 the top of a hill or a mountain. 2 the front part of a cap which sticks out.	**pelican**	a large bird which stores food in a pouch under its beak.
peal	1 the sound made by very large bells ringing. 2 the sound of thunder or laughter.	**pen**	1 a tool which is used when writing with ink. 2 a place fenced in to keep animals together.
peanut	a small, hard, round seed like a nut, used as food.	**penalty**	a punishment for breaking a rule or the law.
pear	a juicy fruit with a greenish-yellow skin and a pointed shape.	**pencil**	a writing-tool made of wood with a grey or coloured centre.
pearl	a precious gem found in some oyster shells.	**penguin**	a large, black and white sea-bird which cannot fly, found near the South Pole.
pebble	a small, smooth, rounded stone.	**penknife**	a small knife with a folding blade.
peck	to pick up food with the beak, to poke at.	**penny**	a small British coin.
peculiar	strange, unusual.	**people**	men, women and children.
pedal	a bar or lever which you move with the feet to drive a machine or play an organ, for example.	**pepper**	a hot-tasting powder which is used for flavouring.
pedestrian	a person who walks.	**peppermint**	a flavouring used in sweets and toothpastes.
peel	1 the outside skin of fruit or vegetables. 2 to take off the skin from (fruit or vegetables.)	**perch**	1 a bar on which a bird can rest. 2 to sit on the edge of something.
peep	to look at quickly and secretly, to glance.	**perfect**	without fault, complete.

perform	to act, to do.
performance	1 something you do, especially in front of an audience. 2 when a play or a ballet, etc. is put on the stage.
perfume	scent, a pleasant smell.
perhaps	maybe, possibly.
period	a length of time.
permanent	not coming to an end, for all time.
permission	being allowed to do something.
permit	to allow, to let someone do something.
persist	to do something again and again, to refuse to stop.
person	a man, a woman or a child.
personal	belonging to a particular person.
perspire	to sweat.
persuade	to talk to a (person) until he or she does as we wish.
pest	a person, an animal or an insect that annoys you or causes damage.
pester	to keep annoying (somebody).
pet	an animal which you keep for pleasure.
petal	one of the usually brightly-coloured separate parts of a flower.

petition	a letter or form, usually signed by a lot of people asking for something.
petrol	the liquid that drives the engine of a motor car.
pew	a seat or bench in a church.
pheasant	a large, colourful game-bird with a long tail.
phone	a telephone.
photocopy	a copy of a page etc. made by photographing it.
photograph	a picture taken using a camera.
phrase	a few words which are part of a sentence.
physical	belonging to the natural world or the body.
pianist	a person who plays the piano.
piano	a large musical instrument played by pressing the keys.
pick	1 to gather. 2 to choose. 3 a pointed metal tool with a wooden handle for making holes in hard ground.
pickles	vegetables etc. kept in vinegar.
picnic	a meal eaten in the open air.
picture	a drawing, a painting or a photograph of something.
pie	fruit or meat cooked in a pastry case.

piece	a part of something larger.
pier	a landing-stage for ships built out into the water.
pierce	to make a hole in (something), to stab.
pig	an animal kept for its meat.
pigeon	a greyish bird which makes a soft noise.
piglet	a baby pig.
pile	a large heap.
pilgrim	a person who travels to visit a holy place.
pill	a small ball of medicine for swallowing.
pillar	an upright post, usually of stone, often used to hold up a part of a building.
pillow	a cushion to rest your head on, especially on a bed.
pilot	1 a person who controls an aeroplane. 2 a person who goes on board a ship to guide it into harbour.
pimple	a small, usually red or yellow, swelling on the skin.
pin	a thin, sharp piece of pointed metal used for holding things together.
pincers	1 a tool with jaws which grip when closed. 2 the claws of a crab or lobster, for example.

pinch	1 to nip tightly with the fingers. 2 a very small amount, of salt, for example.
pine	1 to long for something or somebody very much. 2 a tall tree on which cones grow.
pineapple	a juicy fruit grown in hot countries.
pink	a very light red colour.
pint	a measure of liquid.
pip	a small seed (for example in an apple or an orange).
pipe	1 a tube often made of metal or rubber. 2 a bowl with a stem for smoking tobacco. 3 a musical instrument.
pirate	a sea robber.
pistol	a short handgun, a revolver.
pit	1 a hole in or under the ground. 2 a coal-mine.
pitch	1 a stretch of ground for playing games. 2 to put up (a tent). 3 to throw.
pity	1 feeling sorry for somebody. 2 something you are sorry about.
pizza	a flat Italian pie topped with cheese, tomatoes, etc.
place	1 a position on the earth's surface. 2 a space for something.

plague	a terrible disease which spreads very quickly.	**play**	1 a story which is acted. 2 to enjoy yourself, especially in a game. 3 to make sounds on a musical instrument.
plaice	a flat sea-fish, used as food.		
plain	1 ordinary, simple. 2 easily seen or heard. 3 a flat piece of land.	**pleasant**	delightful, pleasing.
		please	1 to make (somebody) happy. 2 a polite word used when asking for something.
plait (say 'plat')	to twist together, one over another, three or more strands of hair or rope.		
plan	1 a drawing of something. 2 to arrange.	**pleasure**	happiness, joy.
		pleat	a fold which is pressed into clothes.
plane	1 an aeroplane. 2 a tool for smoothing wood.	**plenty**	more than enough.
planet	one of the large bodies, such as the earth, that go round the sun.	**pliers**	a tool with handles and a head for gripping and cutting things.
plank	a long, flat piece of wood.	**plot**	1 the story of a play. 2 a piece of ground. 3 a secret plan.
plant	1 something which grows from roots in the ground. 2 to put (seeds) into soil so that they will grow.		
		plough	a machine for breaking up the soil.
plaster	1 a paste to cover walls which goes white and hard when dried. 2 a covering you put on a cut to protect it.	**pluck**	1 to take the feathers from (a dead bird). 2 to gather (flowers). 3 to pull and then let go, the strings of a guitar, for example.
plastic	a light and strong man-made material used to make many different objects.	**plug**	1 a stopper for a bath or a bowl. 2 a fitting you put into a socket to get electricity.
plate	a flat dish from which you eat food.	**plum**	a soft, red or purple fruit with a large, hard seed called a stone in it.
platform	1 a raised place, usually in a hall. 2 the place in a station where you get on and off trains.	**plumber**	a person who fits and repairs water pipes.
		plump	pleasantly fat.

plunge	to dive in.
plural	numbering more than one.
plus	added to; the sign +.
poach	1 to cook gently in water (for example an egg). 2 to hunt animals or catch fish without permission.
pocket	a bag sewn into your clothes to hold money and things.
pod	a long case on a plant with seeds in it.
poem	a piece of poetry.
poet	a person who writes poems.
poetry	words written in lines of a certain length and often rhyming at the ends.
point	1 the sharp end. 2 to show with a finger. 3 a dot. 4 a place or time.
poison	a substance that can harm or kill you if it gets into your body.
poisonous	containing poison.
poke	to push with a stick or a rod.
polar	connected with the **North Pole** or the **South Pole,** the two points on the earth's surface furthest from the equator.
polar bear	a large, white bear which lives near the North Pole.

pole	a long, rounded stick, a rod.
police	people who make sure that the law is obeyed.
polish	1 to make smooth and bright by rubbing. 2 a substance used for polishing.
polite	well-behaved, well-mannered.
pollen	fine, yellow dust found in flowers.
polythene	a kind of plastic.
pond	a small, usually man-made, lake.
pony	a small horse.
poodle	a kind of dog kept as a pet.
pool	1 a small area of still water. 2 a pond prepared for swimming.
poor	1 not having much money, not rich. 2 not very good.
pop	1 a soft, sudden noise. 2 a kind of modern music, especially popular with young people.
poppy	a plant with large flowers, often red.
popular	well-liked by people.
population	the number of people who live in a particular place.
porch	a shelter over an outside door of a building.

pork	meat from a pig.
porpoise	a sea animal rather like a dolphin.
porridge	a breakfast food made of oatmeal boiled in water.
port	1 a place where ships land their cargo. 2 left-hand side of a ship as you face forward.
portable	able to be carried about.
porthole	an opening in a ship's side to let in air and light.
portion	a part or a share of something.
portrait	a picture of a person.
position	1 the place where something or somebody is. 2 a job.
positive	certain, quite sure.
possess	to have; to own.
possible	able to be done; likely to take place.
post	1 an upright pole fixed in the ground. 2 the system for sending and getting letters. 3 a job, a position.
poster	a large piece of paper with a message printed, drawn or painted on it which is put up in public places.
pot	1 a round container (for example a **jampot** or a **teapot**). 2 a deep container with a handle for cooking.

potato	an oval or round-shaped vegetable which is dug out of the ground.
pottery	pots and dishes etc. made of baked clay.
pouch	a small bag.
pound	1 an amount of British money equal to a hundred pence. 2 a measure of weight equal to 16 ounces. 3 to beat very hard.
pour	1 to make (liquid) flow out of a container. 2 to rain heavily.
powder	dust made by crushing a hard substance.
power	strength, force.
practice	doing something often in order to become better at it.
practise	to do something often in order to become better at it.
praise	to say good things about a person or thing.
pram	a small carriage for a baby or doll.
prawn	a kind of small shellfish.
pray	to speak to God.
prayer	what you say when praying.
preach	to give a religious talk.
precious	very valuable, greatly loved.
prefer	to like one person or thing more than the others.

preparations	things you do to get ready for something or someone.
prepare	to make or get ready.
present	1 a gift. 2 in a place or with people. 3 **at present** now.
present	to hand (something) over to someone else.
presently	in a short time, soon.
preserve	to keep (something) from harm or from going bad.
president	the head of a country or of an organisation.
press	1 to push hard. 2 to make smooth with an iron. 3 a machine for printing.
pretend	1 to act as though you were somebody or something else. 2 to act as though something is true, when it isn't.
pretty	attractive, delightful to see.
prevent	to stop (something) from taking place.
previous	coming before.
prey	a bird or an animal that is hunted.
price	what you must pay to buy something, the cost.
priceless	very valuable.
prick	to make a small hole with something pointed.

prickly	1 having sharp points or thorns like a holly leaf. 2 bad tempered, easily annoyed.
pride	the feeling or belief that you are better than other people in some way.
priest	someone who performs religious ceremonies.
prim	neat; easily shocked; almost too well-behaved.
primary	first; earliest.
prime minister	the head of a government.
primrose	a small, yellow spring flower.
prince	a man or boy in a royal family.
princess	a woman or girl in a royal family.
principal	most important, chief, head.
principle	a rule which we must keep or live by.
print	1 to press letters on to paper by a machine. 2 to write without joining up the letters.
prison	a place where people who have broken the law are kept.
private	belonging to one person or group only.
prize	a reward for winning something.
probably	likely.
problem	a difficult thing to settle or to work out.

procession	an orderly march.
prod	to poke with a stick, for example.
produce	something produced by growing.
produce	1 to bring out; to show. 2 to make.
profit	money that you make when you sell something for more than you paid for it, gain.
program	a number of instructions for a computer which you use to tell it what to do.
programme	1 a list of performers and information about what will happen (for example at a concert or competition). 2 something broadcast on television or radio.
progress	moving forward, getting better.
progress	to go forward, to advance.
prohibit	to forbid, usually by order.
project	1 a plan for something special. 2 a long piece of work (for example finding information about a subject).
promise	to say firmly that you will do something.
prompt	in good time, at the right time.
prong	the sharp spike of a fork.
pronoun	a word used in place of a noun (for example he, she, it).

pronounce	to say a word in a certain way.
proof	what shows or proves something to be true.
propeller	curved blades on a ship or an aeroplane which drive it forward.
proper	correct, right.
property	something which belongs to someone.
prophet	someone who is thought to know what is going to happen in the future.
propose	to suggest; to offer.
prosecute	to accuse someone of a crime in a court of law.
prosper	to do well, to succeed.
protect	to prevent (someone or something) being harmed or damaged.
protest	to say strongly that you are against something.
proud	thinking very well of yourself or something you own.
prove	to show that something is true.
proverb	a short, well-known saying.
provide	to give what is needed, to supply.
prune	a dried plum.
psalm	a Bible poem or song.
public	1 for everybody to use. 2 in open view.
publish	to put into print for sale.

pudding   a soft, cooked food, often a sweet one eaten at the end of a meal.

puddle   a small pool of usually dirty water.

puff   a short burst of breath or smoke.

puffin   a sea-bird with a large, brightly-coloured beak.

pull   to drag something towards you.

pullover   a usually woollen garment for the upper part of the body.

pulp   squashed fruit, vegetables, etc.

pulpit   a raised platform in a church from which a sermon is preached.

pulse   the beating of the heart.

pump   1 to force air or liquid into or along something.
2 a machine which does this.

punch   1 to hit with the fist.
2 to make a hole in something.

punctual   arriving at the exact time.

punctuation   full stops, commas and other marks used in writing.

puncture   a small hole made by something pointed.

punish   to make (someone) suffer for something bad they have done or are thought to have done.

pupil   a person who is being taught, especially in a school.

puppet   a kind of doll which can be made to move by pulling strings or by placing it on the hand like a glove.

puppy   a young dog.

purchase   to buy.

pure   with nothing added.

purple   a colour made by mixing red and blue.

purpose   1 what you mean to do.
2 **on purpose** meaning to do something, not by accident.

purr   the noise made by a cat when it is pleased.

purse   a small bag for holding money.

pursue   to follow, to run after.

push   to press against something to try to move it.

put   to move (something) into a place.

putty   a soft mixture which hardens to hold glass in a frame.

puzzle   1 something which is difficult to understand.
2 a game which has to be worked out.

pyjamas   trousers and jacket top worn in bed.

pylon   a metal tower used to hold up electrical cables.

pyramid	a solid shape with flat sides, square at the bottom and pointed at the top.
python	a large snake which squeezes its victims to death.

Q q

quack	the noise made by ducks.
quaint	unusual, strange, odd.
quality	how good or bad something is.
quantity	an amount.
quarrel	to disagree angrily with someone.
quarry	1 a place where stone is taken out of the ground. 2 an animal that is being hunted.
quarter	one of the four equal parts of something.
quay (say 'key')	a landing-place for ships.
queen	1 a woman who is the ruler of a country. 2 the wife of a king.
queer	strange, odd, peculiar.
quench	1 to end (someone's thirst). 2 to put out (a fire).
query	a question, especially about something you think might be wrong.
question	something that needs an answer.

queue (say 'Q')	a line of waiting people or vehicles.
quick	fast, at great speed, done in a short time.
quiet	with no sound or very little, not loud.
quill	1 a long feather. 2 (long ago) a pen made from such a feather.
quilt	a cover for a bed filled with feathers or other soft material.
quite	1 completely, fully. 2 a little, but not very.
quiver	1 to shake, to tremble. 2 a holder for arrows.
quiz	a game in which a lot of questions have to be answered.
quote	to repeat exactly what someone has said or written.

R r

rabbit	a small, furry animal with long ears and long back legs which lives in holes in the ground.
race	1 a test of speed. 2 people of the same kind or colour.
rack	a frame or bar for holding things.
racket	1 a kind of bat used in tennis, for example. 2 a lot of very loud noise.

radar	a way of helping to guide ships and aeroplanes by using radio waves.
radiator	1 a device that sends out heat. 2 the front part of the engine of a motor car, which cools the engine.
radish	a small, red or white, sharp-tasting vegetable used in salads.
radius	a straight line from the centre to the outside edge of a circle.
raffia	straw made from large leaves, woven into mats and baskets.
raffle	a game of chance used to make money. Tickets with numbers are sold and some numbers win prizes.
raft	a platform of logs made to float on water.
rafter	a beam which holds up a roof.
rag	a piece of old or torn cloth.
rage	great anger, a violent temper.
raid	a sudden, unexpected attack.
rail	a fixed wooden, plastic or metal bar (for example for hanging things on).
railway	1 the rails on which trains run. 2 everything to do with trains.
rain	drops of water falling from the clouds.
rainbow	curved stripes of different colours sometimes seen in the sky in rainy weather.
raise	1 to lift, to move up. 2 to bring up (a family or animals). 3 to collect (money).
raisin	a dried grape.
rake	a garden tool with spikes for scratching the earth, gathering dead leaves, etc.
rally	a large gathering of people (for example a **car rally**).
ram	1 a male sheep. 2 to crash into.
ramble	1 a long country walk. 2 to talk foolishly and without thinking.
ramp	a slope between two different levels.
ranch	a large cattle or sheep farm.
random	**at random** by chance.
range	1 the limit that something can reach. 2 a variety of different things, such as goods in a shop. 3 a row of mountains or hills.
rank	1 a line or row (for example of soldiers). 2 a person's official position (for example a captain in the army).
ransom	a sum of money to buy a prisoner's freedom.
rap	a sharp blow or knock.

rapid   very fast, very quick.

rare   scarce, not often seen.

rascal   *1* a very wicked person.
2 a badly-behaved child.

rash   *1* not thinking enough, doing things too quickly.
2 a large number of spots on the skin.

raspberry   a juicy, red berry.

rat   an animal like a large mouse.

rate   *1* the speed of something.
2 the price which has been fixed.

rather   *1* more willingly, sooner.
2 quite, a little.

rattle   *1* the noise of things being shaken together.
2 a baby's toy that rattles.

rave   to speak wildly, to rage and roar.

raven   a large, black bird of the crow family.

ravenous   very hungry.

ravine   a very deep, steep-sided, narrow valley.

raw   *1* not cooked.
2 cold and wet.

ray   a beam or shaft of light.

razor   a very sharp tool for shaving the skin.

reach   *1* to stretch and touch.
2 to arrive at, to get to.

read   to understand the meaning of written or printed words.

ready   *1* willing to do something.
2 prepared for use.

real   true, not false.

realize   to come to understand (something), especially suddenly.

really   truly.

reap   to cut and gather in (a crop).

rear   *1* the back part.
2 (of a horse) to stand up on the hind legs.
3 to look after (children or small animals) until they are fully grown.

reason   the explanation, the cause.

reasonable   sensible; not asking too much.

rebel   a person who rebels.

rebel   to turn against a leader and stop obeying orders.

recall   *1* to call back.
2 to remember.

receipt   a paper stating that something has been received.

receive   to take, to get something that is given or sent.

recent   just happened.

recipe   a list of instructions telling you how to cook something.

recite   to say aloud from memory.

reckon
1 to count, to add up.
2 to think.

record
1 a disc for playing music or words on a **record-player**.
2 the best that has been done so far (for example in a sport).
3 something written down to tell you what has happened.

record
1 to copy (voices or music) on a disc or tape.
2 to write down.

recorder
a wooden musical instrument played by blowing.

recover
1 to get better after an illness.
2 to get (something) back.

re-cover
to put a new cover on.

recreation
rest or play after you have been working.

rectangle
a flat shape like the shape of this page.

red
the colour of blood.

reduce
to make (something) less or smaller.

reed
a kind of long, thin plant which grows near water.

reef
a line of rocks just below the level of the sea.

reel
1 a cylinder used for winding something on to (for example a **fishing reel**, a **reel of cotton**).
2 a lively Scottish dance.
3 to stagger about.

refer (to)
1 to talk about.
2 to be concerned with.

referee
the person who makes sure that a game is fairly played.

reference book
a book in which one can look things up, such as a dictionary, an atlas.

reflect
1 to show or shine back, like a mirror.
2 to think about something that has happened.

refreshment
something to eat or drink.

refrigerator
a special kind of container for keeping food cold.

refuse
rubbish.

refuse
not to accept; to say 'No'.

regard
to think of in a certain way.

regiment
a large group of soldiers, a part of an army.

region
a part of the world or of a country.

register
a list of names etc. kept for a special purpose.

regret
to be very sorry about.

regular
happening often at the same time; usual.

rehearse
to practise something such as a play or a concert.

reign
1 to rule as a king or queen.
2 the length of time a king or queen reigns.

reindeer	a kind of deer with long horns which lives in cold northern countries.	**removal**	moving from one house to another.
reins	straps used to control and guide a horse etc.	**remove**	1 to take away. 2 to move from one place to another.
relation	someone in the same family.	**rent**	the money you pay for the use of a house, a television set, etc.
relative	someone in the same family.	**repair**	to mend, to put right.
relay	a race in which each person in a team runs or swims a different part of the course.	**repeat**	to do or say (something) again.
		replace	to put back.
release	to allow to go free.	**reply**	to answer.
reliable	able to be trusted.	**report**	a description of something which has happened; a statement of what someone has done.
relic	a thing left from past times, often something holy.		
relief	1 the feeling when pain, fear, or worry stops. 2 help for people in trouble.	**reptile**	an animal with cold blood such as a snake or a lizard.
		request	to ask politely for (something).
religion	a way of believing in God or in gods.	**require**	to need, to want.
religious	to do with religion; following a religion.	**rescue**	to save, to take out of danger.
rely on	to depend on, to count on, to trust.	**reserve**	1 to keep (something) until it is needed. 2 something spare or extra. 3 an area of land set aside for wildlife.
remain	to stay behind.		
remainder	what is left over.		
remark	something said about someone or something.	**reservoir**	a large lake which has been specially made to supply a town or city with water.
remarkable	unusual, worth noting.		
remedy	a cure.	**respect**	to admire, to look up to.
remember	to bring back into the mind; not to forget.	**rest**	1 the others; what is left over. 2 to be still, not to work or do anything tiring.
remind	to make (someone) remember.		

restaurant	a place where you can buy food and eat it there.
restore	1 to give or bring back. 2 to clean and repair.
result	1 what happens because of something. 2 the final score in a sporting contest.
retire	to stop working, usually because you have reached a certain age.
retreat	to go back (especially of an army which is being attacked).
return	1 to go or come back. 2 to give back.
reveal	to show, to make known (especially something hidden).
revenge	the hurt you do to someone in return for something they did to you.
reverse	1 to go backwards. 2 to go in the opposite direction.
revise	1 to read over something and correct and improve it. 2 to look over something again (for example before an exam).
revolt	to turn against a leader.
revolution	a great change, especially a change in the government of a country made by force.
revolver	a kind of small handgun which can fire several bullets without being reloaded.

reward	something you are given for something good or brave you have done.
rhinoceros	a large, thick-skinned animal found mainly in Africa with one or two horns on its nose.
rhubarb	a garden plant with juicy stalks that can be eaten.
rhyme	1 word endings which sound alike. 2 a piece of poetry with rhymes in it.
rhythm	the steady beat or time of poetry or music.
rib	one of the bones across the chest.
ribbon	a narrow band of material (for example for tying things).
rice	a plant grown in hot countries; the grain of this plant is an important food.
rich	1 having a lot of money or other valuable things. 2 of food, having a lot of fat, sugar, etc.
rid	to be free of.
riddle	a word puzzle in which a question has a funny answer.
ride	1 to move about on an animal or a bicycle or in a carriage. 2 a journey or trip on an animal or a bicycle or in a car, bus or other vehicle.
ridiculous	so silly that it may be laughed at.

rifle	a kind of gun with a long barrel.	**roam**	to wander about.
right	1 correct; not wrong. 2 good; true. 3 the opposite of left.	**roar**	a loud, deep sound, the noise made by a lion or by thunder.
rim	the edge of something round, such as a bowl or a wheel.	**roast**	to cook in fat in an oven or over a fire.
rind	the outer covering (for example of an orange, a lemon or a cheese).	**rob**	to take something that does not belong to you, to steal from.
ring	1 a round piece of metal (for example one worn on the finger). 2 a circle. 3 the sound made by a bell.	**robbery**	the act of robbing.
		robe	a long, loose piece of clothing.
		robin	a small, friendly, red-breasted bird.
rink	a place made specially for ice-skating or roller-skating.	**robot**	a machine that can do some of the work a person can do.
rinse	to wash with clean water, usually after washing with soap.	**rock**	1 stone; a large piece of it. 2 to move from side to side. 3 a long, sticky sweet shaped like a stick. 4 a kind of popular music.
riot	fighting and disturbance by a lot of people.		
rip	to tear roughly.		
ripe	fully grown, ready to eat.		
ripple	a tiny wave.	**rockery**	part of a garden with lots of rocks, where certain plants grow well.
risk	the danger of something going wrong.		
rival	a person who tries to equal or to do better than another person.	**rocket**	1 a long tube driven into the air by gas or an explosion. 2 a kind of firework. 3 a spaceship.
river	a long, wide stream of water, usually flowing into the sea.	**rod**	a thin bar of wood or metal.
road	a wide track on which cars, buses, lorries, etc. can travel.	**rogue**	a very wicked person that you cannot trust.

roll
1 to turn over and over.
2 something wrapped round and round itself (for example a **roll** of wallpaper).
3 a long sound made by drums.
4 a small piece of bread, like a small loaf.

roller-skate wheels attached to a boot or shoe to allow you to move along quickly.

roof
1 the top covering of a building.
2 the top part of the inside of the mouth.

rook
1 a black bird of the crow family with a grey beak.
2 a chess piece, also called a castle.

room
1 a part of a building, with its own floor, walls and ceiling.
2 space for something.

root
1 the part of a plant which is in the soil and absorbs water to feed the plant.
2 the beginning or origin of something (for example a problem).

rope a thick cord.

rose a brightly-coloured, sweet-smelling flower, often found in gardens and hedges.

rosehip the fruit of the rose bush.

rosy pink in colour.

rot to go bad (and die).

rotten
1 gone bad.
2 nasty, unpleasant.

rough
1 not smooth; coarse.
2 wild and stormy.
3 (of a drawing, plan, etc.) not in its final state.

round the same shape as a ball or ring.

rounders a game played by two sides with bat and ball.

route the way to go somewhere.

routine doing things in a regular orderly way.

row (rhymes with 'low')
1 a line of people or things.
2 to move a boat with oars.

row (rhymes with 'now') a noisy quarrel.

rowing-boat a boat driven by oars.

royal connected with kings and queens.

rub to move one thing against another many times.

rubber
1 the name of a tree grown in hot countries.
2 elastic material made from the sap of the rubber tree, used for making tyres, keeping out water, etc.
3 a small piece of rubber used for rubbing out writing.

rubbish
1 waste things that are of no use.
2 nonsense.

ruby a deep-red precious stone.

rucksack	a bag you can carry on your back.
rudder	a piece of wood or metal fixed at the back to steer a boat or an aeroplane.
rude	not polite, vulgar.
rug	1 a small carpet; a mat. 2 a kind of blanket, sometimes used to keep the knees warm when sitting down.
rugby	a game played with an oval ball which may be kicked or carried.
ruin	1 a building which has fallen down. 2 to wreck; to spoil.
rule	1 a law that must be followed. 2 to have power over other people.
ruler	1 a person who rules. 2 a strip of wood or other material used for measuring or drawing straight lines.
rumble	a deep roll of sound like the sound of thunder.
rumour	something you hear which may or may not be true.
run	to move very quickly on foot.
rung	a step on a ladder.
rush	1 to move very quickly; to hurry. 2 a kind of long, thin plant which grows near water.

rust	a reddish-brown coating sometimes found on iron and steel.
rustle	a gentle rubbing sound, like paper being moved.
rusty	covered with rust.
rye	a kind of grass. Its grain is made into bread in some countries.

S s

sabbath	the day for the worship of God in the Jewish and Christian religions.
sack	1 a large bag, usually made of rough cloth. 2 to remove (somebody) from a job.
sacred	holy; to do with religion.
sacrifice	the giving up of something that you like very much.
sad	unhappy; miserable.
saddle	the seat of a bicycle; a seat for the rider of a horse.
safari	a journey in Africa to see wild animals or to hunt them.
safari park	a park where you can see wild animals roaming about.
safe	1 not in danger, free from possible harm. 2 a strong, locked metal box used to keep valuable things in.
safety	a safe place.

safety belt	a seat-belt.
sag	to hang or bend downwards, often in the middle.
sail	1 a large piece of strong cloth used on a sailing boat to make it move in the wind. 2 to travel in a boat.
sailor	1 a person who works on a ship. 2 a person who sails a yacht.
saint	a very good and holy person.
salad	a dish of cold, usually raw vegetables etc.
salary	payment for work, usually given at the end of each month.
sale	1 the selling of things. 2 a time when things are sold at a lower price than usual.
saliva	the liquid in your mouth.
salmon	a large fish with pink flesh.
salt	a mineral used to flavour or preserve food.
salute	to greet, especially by raising the hand to the forehead.
same	not different; exactly like.
sample	1 a small piece to show what something is like. 2 to test, try out.
sand	powdered rock or shells often found at the seaside or in the desert.

sandal	an open-topped shoe fastened with straps or cords.
sandwich	two slices of bread with a filling between them.
sane	not mad; sensible.
sap	1 the liquid in the stems of plants and trees. 2 to weaken, to drain energy from (something).
sarcastic	being hurtful to someone by saying something but meaning the opposite.
sardine	a small sea-fish used as food.
sash	1 a long, wide ribbon worn round the waist or over the shoulder. 2 a window-frame.
satchel	a child's schoolbag.
satellite	a natural or man-made body moving in space round a planet.
satin	a kind of smooth cloth with one shiny side, usually made of silk.
satisfy	to make content and happy.
satsuma	a kind of fruit like a small orange.
sauce	a thick liquid food eaten with other food to add flavour.
saucepan	a metal container with a handle used for cooking.
saucer	a small, round plate on which a cup stands.

sausage	a mixture of minced meat, breadcrumbs, fat, etc. in a thin skin.
savage	fierce, wild, cruel.
save	1 to help (someone) to be safe. 2 to keep (something) until you need it. 3 to use less of (something).
savings	money you save up.
saw	a metal cutting-tool with sharp, pointed teeth.
say	to speak, to tell in words.
scab	a hard covering which forms over a wound or spot.
scaffolding	a framework on which builders etc. work.
scald	to burn with hot liquid.
scale	1 a set of numbers or marks for measuring. 2 a set of musical notes going up and down. 3 a small piece of flat shiny material on the skin of a fish or snake, etc.
scales	a machine for weighing things.
scalp	the skin and hair on the top of the head.
scamper	to run quickly and lightly.
scandal	something said or talked about which shocks other people.
scar	a mark left on the skin by a wound.
scarce	not often found because there are not many.

scarcely	hardly at all.
scare	to frighten badly.
scarf	a square or length of cloth used as a covering for the neck and shoulders etc.
scarlet	a very bright red colour.
scatter	1 to throw (something) about in different directions. 2 to move away quickly in different directions.
scene	1 a view. 2 a part of a play. 3 the place where something happened.
scent	1 a pleasant smell, a perfume. 2 the smell an animal leaves behind it.
scheme	a plan.
scholar	a person who has studied a subject a great deal and knows a lot about it.
school	1 a place where people, usually children, go to learn. 2 a large group of fish swimming together.
science	knowledge of and learning about nature and how things are made.
scientist	a person who studies science.
scissors	a cutting tool with two blades fastened together in the middle.
scoff at	to make fun of; to mock.

scold	to talk harshly to (someone) because they have done something wrong.
scorch	to burn (something) slightly, often making it brown, to singe.
score	1 to count points, runs or goals in a game or competition. 2 the number of points, runs, goals, etc. made in a game or competition. 3 (a group of) twenty.
scout	a person who is sent out to find out information (for example about an enemy).
scowl	to give a very angry look, to frown.
scramble	1 to climb or crawl quickly, often over rough ground. 2 to mix up.
scrap	1 a tiny piece. 2 rubbish thrown away. 3 a fight.
scrape	1 to rub and clean with something hard. 2 a difficulty.
scratch	1 to mark or tear slightly with something sharp or pointed. 2 to rub the skin because it is itchy.
scrawl	to write badly, to scribble.
scream	to make a piercing cry, usually because of fear or pain.
screech	a harsh, high sound.

screen	1 a large white surface on which a film is shown; the front viewing part of a television set or computer. 2 a large covered-in frame (used for example as shelter from the cold or to divide up a room).
screw	a nail with grooves round it so that it can be turned by a **screwdriver**.
scribble	to write so quickly and carelessly that the writing can hardly be read.
scrub	to clean with water and, usually, a brush.
scuffle	a struggle with much pushing, a kind of fight.
sculptor	a person who makes artistic shapes out of stone, metal, wood, etc.
sculpture	1 the work of a sculptor. 2 a piece of work by a sculptor.
sea	the salt water which surrounds the land on the earth's surface.
seal	1 a sea animal. 2 to close or fasten tightly (for example an envelope). 3 a design used as the special badge of an important organisation, often stamped into wax.
seam	1 a line of stitches where cloth is joined. 2 a layer of coal etc. under the ground.

search	1 to look very hard in order to find something. 2 **search for** to look for.	**see**	1 what you are able to do with your eyes. 2 to understand.
seasick	feeling sick because of the movement of a boat or ship.	**seed**	a grain from which a plant grows.
		seek	to search for, to look for.
season	1 one of the four main parts of the year: spring, summer, autumn, winter. 2 a special time of year (for example the **festive season**). 3 to add something to (food) to make it taste better.	**seem**	to appear to be.
		seesaw	a plank on which children sit at opposite ends and go up and down.
		seize	to take hold of roughly; to grab quickly.
		seldom	not often; rarely.
seat	something to sit on.	**select**	to choose; to pick out.
seat-belt	a belt you wear in a motor car or an aeroplane to stop you being thrown about if there is an accident.	**selection**	a number of things that have been chosen.
		selfish	thinking only about yourself.
seaweed	plants which grow in the sea.	**sell**	to give (something) to someone else in exchange for money.
second	after the first.	**semicircle**	half of a circle.
secondary school	a school for children between the ages of 11 and 18.	**send**	to make (someone or something) go somewhere.
second-hand	not new, having been owned already by someone else.	**senior**	1 older than others. 2 having a higher position in an organisation or having been there longer.
secret	something known only to a few people.	**sense**	1 the ability to think in a reasonable way. 2 the power to see, hear, smell, taste or touch. 3 a meaning.
secretary	a person whose job it is to write letters, make arrangements, etc. for another person or for an organisation.		
section	a part of something.		
secure	firm, safe, free from danger.	**sensible**	having good sense, reasonable.

sentence
1 a group of words that make sense together.
2 a punishment given by a judge at the end of a trial.

sentry
a soldier on guard at a door or gate.

separate
divided, not joined to something else.

sergeant
(say 'sarjint')
an officer in the police or in the army.

serial
a story told or written in parts.

serious
1 of great importance.
2 causing great harm (for example an illness or a crime).
3 not cheerful or funny.

sermon
a talk given as part of a service in a church.

serpent
a snake.

servant
a person who does work for another person, especially housework.

serve
1 to work for (someone).
2 to give out goods (for example in a shop).
3 to give food to.

service
1 something you do for others.
2 something people can use to help them (for example a **bus service**).
3 a ceremony in church.

set
1 to put (something) in a place.
2 a group of people or things which are alike in some way.
3 a radio or television receiver.

settle
1 to sink to the bottom.
2 to become still or calm.
3 to go to live in a place (for a long time).
4 to fix, decide on.

seven
7, a number.

seventeen
17, a number.

seventy
70, a number.

several
some, a few, not many.

severe
very serious or bad (for example an illness or a frost).

sew
(say 'so')
to join together with stitches using a needle and thread.

sex
one of the two groups, male and female, that people and animals belong to.

shabby
almost worn out.

shade
1 (a place where there is) shelter from the sun or other strong light.
2 the depth of a colour, its lightness or darkness.

shadow
1 a dark part where something is keeping out the light.
2 a dark shape seen where something comes between the light and another surface.

shaft
1 the long handle of a spade, an axe, a golf club, etc.
2 the long part of an arrow, a spear, etc.
3 a long space going up or down (for example into a mine).

shake	to move quickly from side to side or up and down, often because of cold or fear.	**sheep**	an animal kept for its wool and its meat.
shallow	not deep.	**sheet**	1 a large piece of thin cloth often used on a bed.
shame	a feeling of being unhappy because you have done wrong.		2 a thin, flat piece of something (for example paper, glass, metal).
shampoo	a liquid like soap for washing the hair.	**shelf**	a long, flat board fixed to a wall or cupboard, for putting things on.
shape	the appearance or outline of something.	**shell**	1 the hard covering of an egg, a nut, a seed or a snail, and of some sea creatures.
share	1 to divide into parts. 2 to use something along with someone else.		2 a large bullet.
shark	a large, dangerous fish with sharp teeth.	**shelter**	a place where you can be protected from bad weather or danger.
sharp	1 pointed, able to cut, stab or stick into. 2 quick, sudden. 3 able to think, see, hear well and quickly.	**shepherd**	a person who looks after sheep.
		shield	1 to protect from harm. 2 a large piece of metal sometimes held by people to protect themselves when fighting. 3 a prize in the shape of a shield.
shave	to remove hair from the skin with a razor.		
shawl	a covering for the head and shoulders or for wrapping a baby.		
sheaf	a bundle of things tied together, especially newly-cut corn.	**shift**	1 to move. 2 a group of people working in turns with other groups.
shears	large scissors (used for example for cutting hedges, or wool from sheep).	**shin**	the front of the leg between the knee and the ankle.
sheath	a close-fitting cover, especially for a sword or knife.	**shine**	1 to give out light. 2 to look bright, to sparkle.
shed	1 a hut. 2 to let fall or pour out (for example tears, leaves).	**shingle**	small stones on the seashore.
		ship	a very large boat.

shipwreck	the destruction of a ship, often in a storm.
shirt	a garment for the upper part of the body, of light cloth with sleeves and a collar, often worn by men.
shiver	to shake because of cold or fear.
shoal	a large group of fish of the same kind swimming together.
shock	1 a sudden violent surprise or force. 2 to make (someone) feel shock.
shoe	a covering for the foot.
shoot	1 to fire (a weapon). 2 a young growth on a plant. 3 to move very quickly.
shop	a place where things are sold.
shore	the land along the edge of the sea or of a lake.
short	small from end to end, not long, not tall.
shortage	not enough.
shorts	short trousers, with legs stopping above the knee.
shot	the shooting of a gun.
shoulder	the place where the arm joins the body.
shout	to speak or cry out in a loud voice.
shove	to push hard.
shovel	a tool for lifting loose things (for example coal).

show	1 to allow to see. 2 where special things can be seen.
shower	1 a short fall of rain or snow. 2 a place to wash yourself where water sprays down on you from above.
shred	a tiny narrow piece (torn off something).
shriek	a high-pitched scream of pain, surprise or laughter.
shrill	(of a sound) high-pitched.
shrimp	a very small kind of shellfish.
shrink	to become smaller.
shrub	a small tree or bush.
shudder	to shake violently with fear or cold.
shut	1 not open, covered over. 2 to cause to be shut.
shy	afraid to speak; easily frightened.
sick	1 feeling that you will bring up food from the stomach. 2 ill, not well.
side	1 one of the parts or surfaces of something which is not the top, bottom, back or front. 2 a team at games.
siege	the surrounding of a place (by soldiers or police) so that no help or food can reach it.

sieve — an instrument with small holes which lets only liquid and small objects through.

sigh — to make a low sound with a deep breath, especially because you are tired or sad.

sight —
1 being able to see.
2 something seen.

sign —
1 a mark, movement or message which has a meaning.
2 to write your name on.

signal — a sign, sound or light which tells you something (for example a red light telling you to stop).

signature — a person's name written by himself or herself (for example at the end of a letter).

silent — quiet, still, without noise; not saying anything.

silk — a kind of smooth, soft cloth made of thread which comes from a kind of caterpillar called a **silkworm**.

silly — foolish, stupid, not sensible.

silver — a valuable, rather soft, whitish metal (used for example to make jewellery, coins, spoons and forks).

similar — almost the same as something else, like.

simple —
1 plain, without any decoration.
2 easy.

sin — doing something very bad, which is against the laws of your religion.

since —
1 from that time until now.
2 because.

sincere — meaning what you say, honest.

sing — to make music with the voice.

singe — to burn slightly.

single —
1 only one.
2 not married.

sink —
1 to go down slowly, especially in water.
2 a large, fixed basin for washing dishes in a kitchen.

sip — to drink in tiny amounts.

sir — a polite title used in speaking to a man.
Sir a title given to a man.

siren — a long loud warning sound which can be heard for a long distance.

sister — a girl or woman who has the same parents as another person.

sit — to rest on your bottom with your back upright.

six — 6, a number.

sixteen — 16, a number.

sixty — 60, a number.

size — how big something is.

skate —
1 a metal blade fitted to a boot to allow you to move quickly on ice.
2 to move on ice using skates.
3 to move on roller-skates.

skateboard	a flat board on wheels on which you can stand and move about for fun.
skeleton	the framework formed by all the bones in the body.
sketch	to draw quickly and roughly.
ski	1 a long, thin piece of wood, metal or plastic fitted to a boot to allow you to move quickly over snow. 2 to move on snow using skis.
skid	to slide out of control on a slippery surface.
skilful	having skill.
skill	cleverness, ability to do things well.
skin	the outer covering of a person or an animal or of a fruit or vegetable.
skinny	very thin.
skip	1 to move with little jumping steps. 2 to jump over a turning rope.
skirt	a woman's garment that hangs from the waist.
skittle	a wooden block knocked down by rolling or throwing a ball in the game of **skittles**.
skull	the bones that cover your head.
sky	the space above the earth where the sun, moon and stars are seen.
skylark	a small bird which sings when it is flying high in the sky.

slab	a thick, flat piece of something.
slack	1 loose. 2 careless, not working hard.
slam	to bang or shut loudly.
slant	a slope.
slap	a hard smack with the flat of the hand.
slate	1 a kind of grey rock that splits easily into thin pieces. 2 a piece of this used as a tile on a roof.
slaughter	to kill (animals) for food.
slave	a person who is owned by another person and is forced to work for them without pay.
slay	to kill.
sledge	a small vehicle without wheels which moves smoothly on snow.
sleep	to rest with the eyes closed and without being conscious.
sleet	snow and rain falling together.
sleeve	the part of a garment that covers an arm.
sleigh (say 'slay')	a sledge drawn by animals.
slice	a thin piece cut from something larger.
slide	1 to move smoothly along a slippery surface; to slip. 2 a hair fastener. 3 a small photograph for showing on a screen.

slight	1 thin, small, not very strong. 2 small, of no importance.
slightly	a little, a small amount.
slim	1 thin. 2 to become thinner.
sling	1 a bandage to support a broken arm. 2 to throw.
slip	1 to move quickly and quietly. 2 to lose your balance on a smooth surface. 3 to make a mistake. 4 a piece of paper.
slippers	light, soft shoes worn in the house.
slippery	so smooth that you are likely to slide on it.
slit	a narrow cut or tear.
slope	something that is higher at one end than at the other, a slant.
slow	taking a long time, not quick.
slug	a small animal like a snail, but without a shell.
slush	half-melted, watery snow.
sly	not to be trusted, crafty, cunning.
smack	to hit with a flat hand.
small	little, not big; not important.
smart	1 clever, quick to understand. 2 well dressed. 3 to have a stinging feeling.

smash	to break into many pieces.
smear	to spread something dirty, sticky or greasy over something.
smell	1 to know about through your nose. 2 to have a smell.
smile	to show you are amused or happy by stretching the corners of the mouth.
smoke	1 the dark cloud which rises from something burning. 2 to burn tobacco in a pipe or a cigarette.
smooth	flat, even, not rough.
smother	to stop someone breathing by covering the nose and mouth.
smoulder	to burn slowly with a lot of smoke but no flame.
smudge	a dirty mark.
smuggle	to take things secretly into a country without paying tax on them.
snack	a small amount of food, especially if eaten between meals.
snail	a small animal with a shell on its back.
snake	a smooth, legless animal which glides on its body.
snap	1 to bite at something quickly. 2 to break with a sharp noise. 3 to make a sharp noise with the fingers. 4 a photograph.

snare	a trap set for animals.
snarl	1 (of animals) to growl showing the teeth. 2 to speak in an angry way.
snatch	to grab quickly.
sneak	1 to move secretly. 2 a person who tells something bad about someone else secretly, a telltale.
sneer	to speak in a way that shows you do not think much of someone or something.
sneeze	a sudden, noisy rush of air from the nose.
sniff	to smell noisily with quick breaths.
snob	a person who thinks too much about money and position.
snore	to breathe heavily and noisily while asleep.
snow	frozen raindrops which fall in white flakes.
snug	warm, cosy, comfortable.
soak	1 to make very wet. 2 to leave for a time in a liquid.
soap	a fatty substance used with water for washing.
sob	to weep noisily.
sock	a cloth covering for your foot and ankle, and sometimes the lower part of your leg.
socket	a hole into which something fits (for example an electric plug).

sofa	a seat for more than one person, a couch.
soft	1 not hard. 2 gentle, mild, not rough. 3 quiet, not loud.
soil	1 the earth in which plants grow. 2 to make dirty.
soldier	a person whose job it is to fight, a member of an army.
sole	1 the bottom of a foot or of a shoe or boot. 2 a kind of flat-fish.
solemn	very serious.
solid	1 hard, firm, not liquid or gas. 2 not hollow.
solo	1 a piece of music played or sung by one person alone. 2 done by one person alone (for example a **solo** flight in an aeroplane).
solve	to find the answer to.
somersault	to turn over and over, head over heels.
son	a male child of a parent.
song	a piece of music for the voice.
soon	in a short time.
sooner	1 earlier. 2 rather.
soot	the black substance left behind after burning (for example in a chimney).
sore	painful.

sorrow	a feeling of sadness.	**sow** (rhymes with 'now')	a female pig.
sorry	feeling unhappy because you wish you had not done something or that something had not happened.	**space**	1 the distance between things. 2 what is beyond the Earth's atmosphere.
sort	1 a kind, a type. 2 to put into the right order (for example putting things of the same size together).	**spade**	1 a tool for digging soil. 2 one of the four kinds in a pack of playing cards.
soul	the part of a person that is not the body or the mind and is thought to live on after death, the spirit.	**spanner**	a tool which turns a metal nut to tighten or slacken it.
sound	1 something you hear, a noise. 2 strong and healthy, in a good state.	**spare**	1 not in use at present, extra. 2 to give up, to do without.
soup	a food made by boiling vegetables, meat or fish in a lot of water.	**spark**	a tiny piece of burning material.
sour	1 having a sharp, bitter taste like a lemon. 2 (of milk) not fresh.	**sparkle**	to shine with tiny movements of light.
		sparrow	a small, brown bird often seen near houses.
source	a place where something starts (for example a river).	**speak**	to use the voice to say something, to talk.
south	the direction that is on the right as you face the rising sun.	**spear**	a sharp-pointed weapon with a long, thin handle.
souvenir	something you keep to remind you of something (for example a place you visit).	**special**	1 of a kind that is different. 2 made or done for one person or occasion.
sovereign	1 a king or queen. 2 (long ago) a gold coin worth one pound.	**speck**	a tiny spot of something.
		spectacles	glasses (to help you to see better).
sow (rhymes with 'low')	to put (seeds) into the ground so that they will grow.	**spectator**	a person who watches something (for example a football match).

117

speech	speaking, the sounds you make when you speak.
speed	the quickness or slowness with which something is done.
spell	1 to arrange letters one by one to make words. 2 magic words.
spend	1 to give money to pay for something. 2 to use time in doing something.
sphere	a round ball, a globe.
spice	something, such as pepper, used to give food a special taste.
spider	a small, eight-legged creature which weaves a web to catch insects for food.
spike	a pointed object, especially of metal.
spill	to let (a liquid or powder) out of its container, especially by accident.
spin	1 to turn round and round quickly. 2 to make cotton or wool into thread.
spinach	a kind of green vegetable.
spine	the backbone.
spinster	an unmarried woman.
spire	the pointed, upper part of a tower, often of a church.
spirit	1 the soul of a person. 2 a ghost. 3 life, energy.

spit	1 the liquid that forms in the mouth. 2 to force something out of your mouth.
splash	to throw or scatter liquid noisily.
splendid	1 excellent, very good. 2 very grand.
splinter	a small, sharp piece, usually of wood.
split	to crack, to break (something) along its length.
spoil	to ruin, to damage.
spoilt	(of a child) having been given everything you want so that you become badly behaved.
spoke	a thin bar from the centre to the rim of a wheel.
sponge	1 a soft substance which soaks up water, used for washing. 2 a soft, light cake.
spoon	a utensil used for stirring tea, eating pudding, etc.
sport	games played for exercise or pleasure (for example football, tennis).
spot	1 a tiny mark. 2 to notice.
spout	a short tube through which a liquid is poured (for example from a kettle or teapot).
sprain	to injure by twisting badly (for example the ankle or the wrist).
sprawl	to spread out the limbs lazily.

spray	1 thin jets of water.
	2 a small bunch of flowers.
spread	1 to take up more space.
	2 to scatter about.
	3 to cover a surface with something.
spring	1 to jump in the air.
	2 a metal coil.
	3 a place where water appears from below the ground.
	4 the season between winter and summer.
sprinkle	to scatter (liquid or something powdery) in small drops or grains.
sprint	to run quickly for a short distance.
sprout	to begin to grow.
spur	1 a sharp instrument used to make a horse go faster.
	2 to drive (a person or an animal) to further effort.
spy	a person who finds out and passes on information secretly.
squabble	to quarrel noisily about small things.
square	a shape with four equal sides, like this □.
squash	to crush, to squeeze tightly together or into a small space.
squeak	a small, sharp noise like that made by a mouse.
squeal	a long, shrill cry, often caused by pain or joy.

squeeze	1 to press together, to squash.
	2 to press to get something out (for example an orange, a toothpaste tube).
squirm	to twist about, to wriggle.
squirrel	a small wild animal with a bushy tail which lives among trees.
stab	to make a wound with a sharp-pointed weapon.
stable	a building where horses are kept.
stack	a large, tidy pile.
stadium	a large, open-air sports ground with rows of seats.
staff	a group of people who work together in an office, a shop, etc.
stag	a male deer.
stage	1 a platform in a theatre or hall where people act, dance, etc.
	2 a part of a journey etc.
stagger	to sway as you walk, to walk unsteadily.
stain	a mark which spoils something.
stairs	a set of steps leading to another floor in a building.
stale	1 old, not fresh; no longer fit to eat.
	2 no longer interesting.
stalk	1 the stem of a flower or plant.
	2 to track (an animal) quietly.

stall
1 a counter for selling things (for example in a market).
2 a place where a cow, horse, etc. is kept.
3 **the stalls** seats on the ground level of a cinema or theatre.

stallion
a male horse.

stammer
to have difficulty in saying words, to repeat words without meaning to, to stutter.

stamp
1 the little piece of paper stuck on a letter or parcel to show you have paid to have it sent through the post.
2 to put your feet down hard and noisily.

stand
1 to be in an upright position.
2 to rise up.
3 seats under cover at a sports ground.

standard
a level of measurement or ability to be reached.

star
1 one of the tiny-looking bright objects that can be seen in the sky on a clear night.
2 a very famous actor, sportsperson, etc.

starch
1 a white substance found in some foods such as bread, potatoes.
2 some of this substance mixed with water and used to stiffen clothes.

stare
to look at something steadily for a long time.

starling
a noisy bird with dark, shiny feathers.

start
1 to begin.
2 to make a sudden movement.

startle
to surprise or frighten.

starve
to die or to be ill because you are without food.

state
1 the condition of a thing or person.
2 a country or its government.
3 a part of certain countries, such as the **United States of America**.
4 to say in words, either by writing or by speaking.

statement
something said or written down, especially for an important reason.

station
1 a place from which trains or buses begin or stop on a journey.
2 a place from which certain services are carried out (for example a **police station**, a **fire station**).

stationery
writing materials such as notepaper, envelopes, pens.

statue
an image or a likeness in wood or stone.

stay
not to go away, to remain.

steady
firm, not moving, not changing.

steak
a thick piece of meat or fish.

steal
to take something that is not yours, to rob.

steam	the mist or cloud that comes from boiling water etc.
steel	a hard and strong metal which is made from iron.
steep	sloping sharply.
steeple	a pointed tower on top of a church.
steer	to guide (a boat, a motor car, etc.).
stem	the stalk which holds the leaves or flowers of a plant.
step	1 putting your foot forward or back in order to move. 2 a flat place in a staircase or in front of a door, where you put your feet.
stepfather	a man who marries your mother (for example after your father dies).
stepmother	a woman who marries your father (for example after your mother dies).
stereo	a machine for playing tapes and records which has two loudspeakers.
stern	1 strict, harsh towards another person. 2 the back part of a boat.
stew	meat and vegetables cooked slowly in water.
stick	1 a short, thin piece of wood. 2 to fasten or be fastened by something such as glue.
sticky	able to stick to something else.

stiff	difficult to bend.
stile	steps for climbing over a fence or wall.
still	1 not moving, quiet, peaceful. 2 the same now as before.
sting	a sharp pain caused by an insect or a plant.
stir	1 to move (something) round and round with a stick or spoon. 2 to begin to move about.
stirrups	the metal rings etc. into which a horse rider puts his or her feet.
stitch	1 a loop made in sewing or knitting. 2 a sudden pain in the side.
stock	1 a quantity of things or animals. 2 a liquid in which meat etc. is cooked (used for example to make soup).
stocking	a close-fitting covering for the leg and foot, often made of nylon or wool.
stomach	the part of the body into which food goes after being eaten.
stone	1 the hard material found on and below the surface of the earth; a piece of this. 2 a precious jewel. 3 a hard seed found in some kinds of fruit. 4 a measure of weight equal to 14 pounds.

stool	a seat without a back.
stoop	to bend the body forward.
stop	to end doing something.
store	1 a place for keeping things. 2 to save (something) for later. 3 a large shop.
storey	one floor of a building.
stork	a very large bird with long legs and a long, straight beak.
storm	1 rough weather with wind and rain. 2 to rage at someone.
story	something that is told, especially about things that happen.
stout	fat.
stove	something that produces heat for cooking or heating.
straight	without a bend or turning.
strain	1 to pull or try as hard as you can; to try too hard. 2 to hurt (a muscle).
strainer	an instrument with small holes for letting liquids through, a sieve.
strange	unusual, odd, remarkable.
stranger	a person you do not know; a person who does not know the district.
strap	a long, thin piece of leather etc. (for example for fastening things together).

straw	1 the stalks of wheat, barley, etc. 2 a thin tube for drinking through.
strawberry	a kind of soft red fruit which grows on very small plants.
stray	1 to wander away, to get lost. 2 an animal which wanders because it has no home.
stream	1 a small river. 2 a number of people etc. moving steadily along.
street	a road with buildings along its sides.
strength	being strong, power.
stretch	to make longer or wider by pulling.
stretcher	a frame to carry an injured or sick person lying down.
strict	1 firm, severe. 2 exact.
stride	a long pace or step.
strike	1 to hit something hard. 2 (of a clock) to make a ringing sound. 3 when workers refuse to work.
string	thin cord.
strip	1 a long, narrow piece of something (for example cloth or paper). 2 to undress; to uncover.
stroke	to pass the hand gently over.

stroll	to walk along slowly.
strong	powerful, able to do difficult things with the body, for example lifting heavy things.
structure	1 a building or framework. 2 the way something is made up or organised.
struggle	1 to fight, especially to get free of someone or something. 2 to try very hard to do something.
stubborn	not giving way easily, obstinate.
student	a person who is studying, especially in a college or university.
stuff	1 things, materials. 2 to fill (something) very full.
stuffy	having little fresh air.
stumble	to fall or almost fall, especially by catching the foot on something.
stump	1 the part of a tree which is left when the tree has been cut down. 2 an upright stick used to bowl at in cricket.
stun	1 to amaze or shock (someone). 2 to strike (a person) until he or she is unconscious.
stupid	having no sense, foolish, silly.
sturdy	strong, well built, healthy.
stutter	to stammer.

sty	1 a place where pigs are kept. 2 a small, painful swelling on the eyelid.
style	1 a way of doing, saying or making something. 2 a fashion (for example in dress).
subject	1 what is being talked about. 2 a person who belongs to a country.
submarine	a ship which can go along under water.
substance	something of which things are made, material.
subtract	to take one thing away from another.
succeed	1 to manage to do what you try to do; to do well. 2 to come after, to follow.
suck	1 to take into the mouth by breathing inwards. 2 to move (something, such as a sweet) about in your mouth without chewing it.
sudden	quick, not expected.
suffer	to feel great pain, sorrow, etc.
sufficient	enough, as much as is needed.
sugar	a sweet substance made from sugar canes or beet.
suggest	to say what might be done, to hint.

suit	1 a set of clothes (for example a jacket with trousers or skirt). 2 to be good or right for, to fit.	**supply**	1 to provide the things that are needed. 2 a quantity or store of things.
suitable	correct, just right for something.	**support**	1 to help (someone) by giving what is needed. 2 to hold up. 3 to provide, especially money, for.
suitcase	a container with a handle and stiffened sides for carrying clothes and other belongings.	**suppose**	to think; to believe something to be true.
sulk	to show you are in a bad mood by not saying anything, to take the huff.	**sure**	certain; not having any doubt.
sum	1 something to be worked out with numbers. 2 to add numbers and find the total.	**surface**	1 the outside of something. 2 the area at the top of something (for example water).
summer	the warmest season of the year, between spring and autumn.	**surgeon**	a doctor who carries out operations.
summit	the top, especially of a mountain.	**surgery**	a place where doctors and dentists work.
sun	the large ball of fire in the sky which gives the earth light and heat.	**surname**	the family name, your last name.
sunrise	the time when the sun first appears in the morning.	**surprise**	1 something you did not expect. 2 the feeling that this causes, a shock.
sunset	the time when the sun goes down at night.	**surrender**	to give in, especially to an enemy.
supermarket	a large shop where customers serve themselves.	**surround**	to be all round.
supersonic	faster than the speed of sound.	**suspect**	a person who is suspected.
supper	a meal eaten in the evening.	**suspect**	to believe, to have reason to think, especially something bad (about a person).

swallow
1 to take in, especially food and drink, through the throat.
2 a kind of small bird with pointed wings and a long, forked tail.

swamp   soft, wet ground, a marsh.

swan   a large white water-bird with a long neck.

swap   to exchange.

swarm   a large number of insects moving together.

sway   to move from side to side.

swear
1 to use bad words.
2 to promise faithfully.

sweat   liquid coming through the skin, when you are too hot.

sweater   a woollen garment for the upper part of the body.

sweep
1 to clean (something) with a brush.
2 a person who cleans chimneys.

sweet
1 pleasant to taste, like sugar.
2 a small piece of sweet food such as chocolate, toffee, etc.
3 a sweet dish you eat at the end of a meal, a pudding.
4 kind, charming, nice.

swell   to become bigger.

swelling   a part which becomes bigger, especially on the body.

swerve   to move sideways quickly, especially to avoid something.

swift
1 very fast, very speedy.
2 a kind of small bird with long, narrow wings.

swim   to move along in water by moving parts of the body.

swing
1 to move round from a fixed point, to sway.
2 a moving seat on ropes.
3 a ride on a swing.

switch   a device for turning electrical things off and on.

sword   a metal weapon like a long, sharp, two-sided knife.

sycamore   a kind of tree with large leaves.

syllable   a part of a word which can be pronounced by itself.

syrup   sugar boiled in water to make a thick, sticky, sweet liquid.

system
1 a way of putting things in order.
2 a group of people or things working together.

Tt

tabby
1 a female cat.
2 a cat with greyish or brownish stripes.

table
1 a flat piece of furniture which stands on legs.
2 a list of numbers, facts, etc. in order.

tablet	a pill of medicine.	**tame**	not wild; friendly; not exciting.
tack	1 a small nail with a large head. 2 to fasten things together by using long stitches. 3 to change the direction of a sailing-boat.	**tan**	1 a light-brown colour, especially the colour of your skin after you have been in the sun a lot. 2 to make animal skins into leather.
tackle	1 to try to do (something). 2 to try to take the ball from another player (for example in football). 3 the things which are necessary to do something (for example **fishing-tackle**).	**tandem**	a two-seater bicycle.
		tangerine	a kind of small, sweet orange.
		tangle	a jumble, a muddle, especially of twisted threads, hair, etc.
tadpole	a small black water animal with a long tail which becomes a frog or toad.	**tank**	1 a container to hold large amounts of liquid or gas. 2 a large vehicle which is used in war and is able to move over very rough country.
tag	1 a label. 2 a children's chasing game.	**tanker**	a ship or lorry which carries liquids such as petrol or oil.
tail	the part of a creature that sticks out at the back.	**tap**	1 a knob or handle which is turned to allow liquids to flow. 2 a tiny knock.
tailor	a person who makes clothes such as suits and coats.		
take	1 to get hold of. 2 to carry away. 3 to swallow (medicine, for example).	**tape**	1 a narrow piece of cloth, often used to hold things together. 2 a long, narrow strip of plastic material used for recording.
tale	a story.	**taper**	1 a thin piece of wax candle. 2 to become thin at one end.
talent	something a person is able to do well; an ability.		
talk	to speak, to say something.		
tall	bigger in height than usual.	**tape recorder**	a machine for making a copy of music or words and playing them back.

tapestry	pictures or patterns in silk or cotton worked on heavy cloth.
tar	a thick, black liquid, used in making roads, for example.
target	something at which you aim.
tart	1 a piece of pastry with jam, fruit, etc. in it. 2 sharp, sour to the taste.
tartan	woollen cloth with a pattern of stripes and squares, often used in Scotland for making kilts, for example.
task	a piece of work which has to be done, a job.
tassel	a hanging bunch of threads often used as a decoration.
taste	1 the flavour of food or drink. 2 to try a little of (some food or drink).
tasty	nice to eat, nice-tasting.
tax	money which has to be paid to the government by the people.
taxi	a car that can be hired by paying the driver.
tea	a hot drink made from the dried leaves of a bush grown in eastern countries.
teach	to help to learn, to give lessons to.
teacher	a person who teaches.

team	1 a number of people who work or play together. 2 a number of animals working together.
tear (say 'teer')	a drop of water from the eyes.
tear (say 'tare')	to pull apart, to rip.
tease	to make fun of.
teenager	a person aged between thirteen and nineteen years old.
telegram	a message sent quickly by British Telecom by electrical signals.
telephone	an instrument which carries the sound of someone's voice by wire, using electricity.
telescope	an instrument which you look through to see things that are far away.
television	a machine with a screen on which pictures that are sent by radio waves are seen.
tell	to give news or information in words, to say.
temper	1 the state of the mind, the mood you are in. 2 when you are very angry or annoyed about something.
temperature	the amount of warmth or cold.
temple	1 a large church in some religions. 2 the part of the head between the forehead and the ear.

tempt	to persuade (someone) to try to do what they really do not wish to do or ought to do.
ten	10, a number.
tend	1 to look after. 2 to be likely to.
tender	1 gentle, kind, showing love. 2 not tough, soft. 3 feeling painful.
tennis	a game played by two or four people who use rackets to hit a ball over a net.
tent	a waterproof shelter held up by poles and ropes, used when you are camping.
term	1 a part of the school or college year. 2 a period of time.
terminal	1 a building at an airport where passengers arrive and depart. 2 a place in a town where you can take a bus to an airport. 3 a part of a computer which receives and gives information.
terminus	the place where a railway or bus route ends.
terrace	1 a flat, raised piece of ground. 2 a row of houses joined together.
terrible	very bad.
terrier	a kind of small dog.
terrific	1 very great. 2 very good, excellent.

terrify	to frighten badly, to fill with fear.
territory	a large area of land.
terror	great fear, great fright.
test	to try out (for example by looking at carefully, to examine).
tether	to fasten (an animal) by means of a rope etc.
thank	to say that you are pleased about something that someone has given to you or done for you.
thatch	roof covering made of straw or reeds.
thaw	warmer weather which melts snow and ice.
theatre	1 a building where plays are acted, for example. 2 a room in a hospital where operations take place.
theft	stealing, robbing.
thermometer	an instrument that measures heat and cold.
thick	1 not thin, wide, deep. 2 with a lot of things close together. 3 (of a liquid) not flowing easily.
thief	a person who steals.
thigh	the part of the leg between the hip and the knee.
thimble	a hard covering worn on the finger to protect it when you are sewing.
thin	1 narrow, not fat. 2 (of a liquid) flowing easily.

think	to use the mind; to believe.
third	1 coming after the second.
	2 one of three equal parts.
thirsty	needing or wanting to drink.
thirteen	13, a number.
thirty	30, a number.
thistle	a wild plant with prickly leaves and purple flowers.
thorn	a prickle or point on a plant stem.
thorough	1 taking great care that everything is done.
	2 complete.
thought	thinking; an idea in the mind.
thousand	1000, a number.
thread	a very thin line of material used in sewing, knitting or weaving.
threat	saying or showing that you mean to harm or punish someone.
three	3, a number.
thrilling	very exciting.
throat	the front part of the neck, containing the tubes through which you swallow and breathe.
throb	a strong, steady beat.
throne	a special chair (for example for a king or queen).

through	1 from one side to the other; from one end to the other.
	2 because of.
throw	to make (something) move through the air from your hand.
thrush	a brown songbird with a spotted breast.
thrust	1 to push hard.
	2 the lifting power of an engine (for example of a rocket).
thud	the noise of something falling or bumping heavily.
thumb	the shortest and thickest finger of the hand.
thump	1 a heavy blow, usually struck with the fist.
	2 a dull noise made by this.
thunder	the crash of noise that follows lightning.
tick	1 a mark ✓ to show for example that something has been checked.
	2 the small, regular sound made by a clock or watch.
ticket	a card or paper allowing you to go into a place or to travel by train, plane or bus.
tickle	to touch (someone) lightly and so to make them laugh.
tide	the rising and falling of the sea twice each day.
tidy	neat and in good order, properly arranged.

tie
1 a narrow piece of cloth worn round the neck.
2 to fasten (for example by making a knot).
3 to be equal in a competition or test.

tiger
a fierce Asian animal of the cat family with black and orange striped fur.

tight
fixed or fitting closely together.

tights
a close-fitting garment covering the feet, legs and lower part of the body.

tile
a flat piece of baked clay, plastic, etc. used to cover roofs, floors or walls.

till
1 until.
2 a drawer for holding money in a shop.

tilt
to lean to one side.

timber
wood for making things.

time
1 the passing of minutes, hours, days, months, years.
2 a moment in this or a part of it.

timid
easily frightened, likely to be afraid, shy.

tin
1 a silvery-white metal.
2 a metal can.

tingle
a prickly feeling often caused by cold, fear or excitement.

tinkle
a sound like that of a small bell.

tinsel
glittering material used for decoration.

tiny
very, very small.

tip
1 the pointed end of something.
2 to upset (something).
3 to give money for something done.

tired
1 feeling that you need to rest, usually because you have done a lot.
2 bored.

tissue
1 a piece of soft paper for wiping.
2 very thin paper used for wrapping.

title
1 the name of a book, a play, a piece of music, etc.
2 the first part of a name which shows the person's rank (for example **Lord** Nelson).

toad
an animal like a large frog with a rough skin.

toadstool
a kind of plant shaped like a small umbrella (many of them are poisonous).

toast
bread which has been made crisp and brown by heat.

tobacco
a plant from which the leaves are taken and used for smoking.

toboggan
a light sledge for sliding on snow, especially down slopes as a game.

today
this day.

toddler
a very young child who is just beginning to walk.

toe
one of the five end parts of the foot.

toffee
a sticky sweet made from sugar and butter.

toilet
1 a large bowl used for waste matter from the body.
2 a room with a toilet.

tomato a soft, round, red fruit, often eaten in salads.

tomb a grave.
(rhymes with 'room')

tomorrow the day after today.

ton a large measure of weight.

tone
1 the sound of the voice used in speaking or singing; the sound of a musical instrument.
2 a shade of colour.

tongue the thick, soft part inside the mouth used for tasting, eating and speaking.

tonight this night.

tonne a large measure of weight, equal to 1000 kilograms.

tonsils two small lumps at the back of the throat.

too
1 also.
2 more than enough.

tool an instrument used to help you to do some work.

tooth one of the hard parts growing out of the jaw, used for biting and chewing.

toothache a pain in a tooth.

top
1 the highest part, above all others.
2 a covering or lid for something (for example a bottle).
3 a toy which spins.

topic something you write or talk about.

topple to make or become unsteady and fall over.

torch
1 an electric light which can be carried about.
2 a burning stick carried to give light.

torment great pain and suffering.

torment to cause pain to someone, to tease, to annoy.

torpedo a weapon which can be fired through water, usually against ships.

tortoise a slow-moving animal with a hard, round shell.

torture to cause great pain to someone on purpose.

toss to throw into the air.

total everything added together, the whole.

totter to move unsteadily, to stagger.

touch
1 to be as close as possible to something.
2 to feel gently with the hand or another part of the body.

tough hard, strong; not easy to bite or cut.

tour a journey in which you visit a number of places.

tourist — a person who travels for pleasure.

tow — to pull (something) along using a rope or chain (for example a car or a boat).

towards — in the direction of.

towel — a piece of cloth for drying wet things.

tower — a tall, narrow building or part of a building.

town — a large number of buildings grouped together, smaller than a city but larger than a village.

toy — something you play with.

trace
1 a very small amount left behind.
2 to copy exactly by following the lines of a drawing etc. through transparent paper.
3 to find after searching and following clues.

track
1 a narrow path.
2 a place specially prepared for races.
3 the metal lines on which a train runs.
4 a mark left by a foot or a tyre, for example.

track suit — loose trousers and top sometimes worn over sports clothes.

tractor — a strong machine for towing heavy loads, used especially on a farm.

trade
1 buying and selling.
2 a job, especially one in which you use your hands.

traffic — movement of vehicles and people.

tragedy
1 something very sad that happens.
2 a serious play with a sad ending.

trail
1 to follow a track or the scent of (an animal).
2 to drag or be dragged behind.

trailer
1 a cart or box on wheels which is pulled by a car or lorry.
2 a short piece of a film or video to make you interested in the full film or video.

train
1 railway coaches joined to an engine.
2 the back part of a dress which trails on the ground.
3 to prepare (yourself or someone else) for a job or a sport, for example.

traitor — a person who tells secret things to the enemy and betrays his or her country.

tramp
1 a person with no home who wanders about begging.
2 to walk heavily.

trample — to walk heavily on, often doing damage.

trampoline — a large frame with springs covered with material on which you can bounce up and down.

translate — to change from one language into another.

transparent — able to be seen through.

transport — the moving (of things or people) from place to place.

trap —
1 a device for catching animals, birds, etc.
2 to catch in a clever way.

trapeze — a bar joining two ropes which hang down to make a swing in a circus or a gym.

travel — to move from one place to another.

trawler — a fishing boat which catches fish by dragging a large net in the sea.

tray — a flat piece of wood, plastic or metal for carrying small things.

treacle — a dark, sweet, sticky liquid made from sugar.

treason — the crime of betraying your country.

treasure — a thing or a number of things of great value.

treasurer — a person who looks after the money which belongs to a group of people.

treat —
1 to behave or act towards.
2 something specially pleasant you are given.

tree — a large plant with a trunk, branches and leaves.

tremble — to shiver, to shake with excitement, fear or cold.

trench — a ditch dug in the earth for a special purpose.

trespass — to go into private places without permission.

trial —
1 a test.
2 an examination before a judge to decide whether or not a person is guilty.

triangle —
1 a flat shape with three straight sides and three corners, like this △.
2 a metal musical instrument of this shape, played by striking it with a steel rod.

tribe — a group of people ruled by one chief.

trick —
1 to cheat.
2 something clever done either to cheat or to amuse people.

trickle — a very small flow of a liquid.

tricycle — a cycle with three wheels.

trifle —
1 a small thing of no importance.
2 a kind of dessert made of cake, fruit, cream, etc.

trigger — a small lever which is pulled to fire a gun.

trim —
1 tidy, neat.
2 to cut and make tidy.

trio — a group of three people doing something together (for example singing or playing instruments).

trip —
1 a journey, especially one for pleasure.
2 to stumble and fall.

triplet — one of three babies born at the same time to the same mother.

triumph — a great victory or success.

trolley
1 a small, light cart pushed by hand.
2 a small table on wheels for serving food.

trombone
a long, brass musical instrument which you play by blowing.

troop
a group of people (for example soldiers).

troops
soldiers.

tropical
of or like the tropics, very hot.

tropics
the part of the world near the equator.

trot
to run gently with short steps.

trouble
1 a worry, a problem, a difficulty.
2 to cause worry or annoyance to.

trousers
a piece of clothing for the legs and the lower part of the body.

trout
a kind of fish that lives in fresh water, used as food.

trowel
1 a garden tool like a small spade.
2 a small, flat-bladed tool for spreading cement, for example.

truant
a person who stays away from school without permission.

truck
a vehicle for carrying heavy loads.

trudge
to walk slowly and heavily as you do when you are tired.

true
correct, honest.

trumpet
a brass musical instrument which you play by blowing.

trunk
1 the thick stem of a tree.
2 a large box for carrying things, especially on a journey.
3 an elephant's long nose.
4 the body (without the head, arms and legs).

trunks
very short trousers worn by men and boys for swimming etc.

trust
1 to believe that someone is honest and can be relied on.
2 to believe to be true.

truth
what is true.

try
1 to make an effort to do something.
2 to test.

tub
a large, round container with an open top.

tube
1 a thin pipe.
2 a soft, metal or plastic container from which things such as toothpaste can be squeezed.
3 an underground railway, especially in London.

tuck
to push or put (something) into or under something.

tuft
a small bunch of grass, hair, feathers, etc.

tug
1 to pull hard and sharply.
2 a small, powerful boat used to pull other boats.

tulip a bell-shaped, spring flower grown from a bulb.

tumble to fall heavily.

tumbler a flat-bottomed drinking glass.

tuna a very large fish found in warm seas, used as food.

tune a set of pleasant musical notes.

tunnel a long covered passageway through hills or under rivers.

turban a head-covering made from a long strip of material wound in a special way round the head.

turf short grass with its roots and the earth in which it grows.

turkey a large bird used as food.

turn
1 to face a different way; to move round.
2 to change.
3 a chance to do something after other people (for example in a game).

turnip a root vegetable with white or yellowish flesh.

turquoise
1 a greenish-blue precious stone.
2 the colour of this.

turret a small tower in a building.

turtle an animal with a hard, round shell which lives mainly in the sea.

tusk a long, pointed tooth found in some animals such as an elephant or a walrus.

tweed a kind of rough, woollen cloth, used for suits and heavy coats, for example.

tweezers a small tool for getting hold of things.

twelve 12, a number.

twenty 20, a number.

twice two times.

twig a very small branch of a tree.

twilight dim light just after sunset.

twin one of two babies born at the same time to the same mother.

twine thin, strong string.

twinkle to shine with small, bright flashes.

twirl to twist round, to spin quickly.

twist
1 to wind things round each other.
2 to turn (a bottle cap, for example).

twitch to move suddenly and quickly.

twitter chirping sounds, like those made by birds.

two 2, a number.

type
1 a special sort, a kind.
2 to tap keys on a typewriter or keyboard in order to print words.

typewriter   a machine with a keyboard used to print words on paper.

typhoon   a great storm.

tyre   the rubber round the outside of a wheel, often filled with air.

U u

ugly   not nice to look at.

umbrella   a covering you hold over your head to keep off the rain.

umpire   the person who makes sure that a game is played fairly, a referee.

uncle   the brother of a father or mother; an aunt's husband.

uncommon   unusual.

unconscious   not conscious; not knowing what is happening.

uncover   to take the lid or covering off (something).

under   below.

underground   1 under the earth.
2 a railway which goes under the ground.

undergrowth   the thick plants or grasses which grow under or around trees.

understand   to know what something means.

underwear   clothes worn next to the skin under other clothes.

undo   to untie.

unemployed   having no paid work.

unfair   not fair.

unfold   to open out something folded.

unfortunate   having bad luck.

unhappy   not happy.

unicorn   an imaginary animal like a horse, with one long horn.

uniform   special clothing worn by people of the same group, such as policemen, soldiers or nurses.

union   a joining together.

unique   the only one of a kind.

unit   1 one complete thing or set.
2 an amount used as a measurement.
3 a number under ten.

unite   to join together into one.

universe   all the suns and planets in space.

university   a place where people may go to learn after leaving school.

unless   if not; except if.

unload   to take something off (a lorry, for example).

unlock   to open with a key.

unnecessary   not needed.

unpack   to take things out of a case or container.

unruly   out of control, badly behaved.

untie   to loosen a knot (for example in string).

until	up to the time of, till.
unwell	ill.
up	to a higher place.
upon	on, on top of.
upper	higher.
upright	1 standing straight up. 2 honest and trustworthy.
uproar	a lot of loud noise and excitement.
upset	1 to make (others) unhappy. 2 to turn over, to knock down.
upside-down	the wrong way up.
upwards	up to a higher place.
urge	to try to get (somebody) to do a certain thing.
urgent	of great importance so that it needs to be done at once.
use (say 'yooz')	to do something with.
use (say 'yoos')	having purpose, being used.
useful	of some use, helpful.
useless	of no use, not useful.
usual	often done; happening often.
utensil	a useful tool or container, especially in the kitchen.
utmost	1 the most that is possible. 2 the greatest.
utter	1 to speak. 2 complete.

V v

vacant	empty.
vacuum	1 a space with no air in it. 2 **vacuum cleaner** a machine for lifting dirt out of carpets, for example. 3 **vacuum flask** a container for keeping liquids hot, usually.
vague	not certain or clear.
vain	1 too proud, conceited. 2 **in vain** uselessly.
valley	low ground between two hills or mountains.
valuable	worth a lot.
value	the importance you put on something, its price.
valve	an instrument to control a flow of water, air or electricity.
van	1 a covered lorry. 2 a railway coach for luggage and parcels.
vanilla	a sweet flavouring used in ice-cream, for example.
vanish	to go out of sight, to disappear.
vapour	liquid in the form of mist, steam or cloud.
variety	1 many different things mixed together. 2 a kind.
various	of several different kinds.
varnish	a substance painted on a surface to make it shiny.

vase — a container for holding flowers.

vast — very large, of great size.

veal — meat from a calf.

vegetable — a plant grown for food (for example carrot or cabbage).

vegetarian — a person who does not eat meat or fish.

vehicle — something such as a cart, car or van used for carrying people or goods.

veil — a thin covering for the face or head, usually to hide it.

vein — one of the thin tubes which carry blood round the body to the heart.

velvet — a kind of cloth which is soft and smooth on one side.

verb — a word which says what someone or something does or is.

verdict — what is decided, especially in a law court.

verge — the edge of a road or path.

vermin — small, harmful animals or insects.

verse —
1 poetry.
2 part of a poem.
3 a small section from the Bible.

version — one person's description of what has happened.

versus — against (another team, for example).

vertical — straight up, standing upright, at right angles to the horizon.

vessel —
1 a container for liquids.
2 a ship.

vest — a garment worn next to the skin on the top part of the body.

vet — an animal doctor.

vibrate — to shake, to throb.

vicar — (in the Church of England) a priest who is in charge of a church or parish.

vice —
1 evil; badness.
2 a fixed tool which grips things to stop them from moving.

vicious — very bad, very wicked.

victim — a person who has suffered because of what other people have done to him or her or because of illness or an accident.

victory — when a person or a group of people beats others in battle or in a competition.

video —
1 a film for showing on a television set.
2 a machine which records and plays back films and television programmes.

view —
1 what you can see.
2 what you think about something.

vigorous — strong, active.

village — a number of houses grouped together, a small town.

villain	a wicked person, a rascal.
vine	a plant on which grapes grow.
vinegar	a sour liquid used for flavouring and for preserving food.
violence	1 great force. 2 wild, hurtful behaviour.
violet	1 a tiny, bluish-purple flower. 2 a bluish-purple colour.
violin	a stringed musical instrument held under the chin and played with a bow.
virtue	goodness.
virus	a very small living thing in the blood that often causes illness.
visible	able to be seen.
vision	1 sight. 2 something seen in a dream.
visit	to call to see (someone or something).
vital	necessary for life, very important.
vitamin	a substance living things need in small amounts to help them to stay healthy.
vivid	bright and clear.
vixen	a female fox.
vocabulary	the words used in speaking and writing.
voice	the sound made by the mouth when speaking or singing.

volcano	a mountain which throws out melting rock, hot ashes, steam and flames.
volleyball	a game in which a ball is played back and forward over a net by hand.
volume	1 the space something fills. 2 a book. 3 how loud a sound is.
voluntary	done freely and openly.
volunteer	a person who offers to do something.
vomit	to be sick.
vote	to make a choice, to choose at an election.
vow	a solemn promise.
vowel	the letter **a**, **e**, **i**, **o** or **u**.
voyage	a long journey, usually by sea.
vulgar	rude, not polite.
vulture	a large, powerful, flesh-eating bird.

W w

waddle	to walk like a duck.
wade	to walk through water.
wafer	a thin biscuit often eaten with ice-cream.
wag	to move (something) from side to side.
wage	money given for work done, often paid weekly.

wagon	1 a four-wheeled vehicle which carries heavy loads. 2 a railway truck.
wail	to cry in sorrow.
waist	the middle of the body, just above the hips.
wait	to stay in a place for a reason.
waiter	a man who serves food in a restaurant or café.
waitress	a woman who serves food in a restaurant or café.
wake	1 to stop sleeping. 2 the foam made in the sea behind a ship.
walk	to move on the feet.
wall	a barrier or part of a building made of bricks or stones.
wallet	a small, flat case for money and cards, usually carried in the pocket.
walnut	1 a kind of nut. 2 the tree it grows on; the wood is used for making furniture.
walrus	a water animal like a large seal with two long tusks.
waltz	a graceful dance for two people.
wand	a thin, straight stick used by magicians.
wander	to roam about.
want	to wish to have.
war	fighting between countries or large groups of people.
ward	a room at a hospital with, usually, a lot of beds.
warden	a person who looks after a building where people live.
warder	a man who looks after prisoners in a jail.
wardrobe	a cupboard for storing clothes.
warehouse	a large building where goods are stored.
warm	fairly hot.
warn	to tell beforehand of difficulty or danger.
warrior	a fighter, a soldier.
wart	a small, hard lump on the skin.
wash	to clean using water.
wasp	a black-and-yellow striped insect with a painful sting.
waste	1 useless things. 2 to spoil or use carelessly.
watch	1 a small clock, usually worn on the wrist. 2 to look at carefully. 3 to guard.
watchman	a man who looks after a place.
water	the liquid that is found in rivers and in the sea and falls as rain.
waterfall	a stream or river falling from a height.
waterproof	made of material through which water cannot go.

wave	1 a higher part of the moving surface of water. 2 to move the hand and arm from side to side. 3 a curl in your hair.	**weep**	to have tears in your eyes, to cry.
wax	a substance which melts easily, used to make candles, for example.	**weigh**	1 to measure how heavy something is. 2 to be a certain weight.
		weight	how heavy something is.
		weird	very strange.
way	1 how you do something. 2 a road or path.	**welcome**	to show you are happy because someone has come.
weak	not strong.	**welfare**	happiness, good health.
wealthy	having a lot of money.	**well**	1 a deep hole holding water or oil.
weapon	something you use to fight or hunt with.		2 in good health. 3 in a good way.
wear	1 to have (clothes) on. 2 to become damaged by a lot of use.	**wellingtons**	long, rubber boots.
weary	very tired.	**west**	the direction where the sun sets.
weasel	a small, furry animal with a long body which hunts birds, mice, etc.	**wet**	having a lot of liquid in it or on it.
		whale	the largest sea animal.
weather	the kind of day it is (for example sunny, cold or wet).	**wheat**	a plant producing grain which is used to make flour etc.
weave	to make cloth by twisting threads over and under each other.	**wheel**	1 a ring of metal, plastic, etc. which turns on its centre (for example on a car or bicycle).
web	the thin net made by a spider to catch flies.		2 to push something that has wheels.
wedding	when two people get married.	**whimper**	to cry softly.
wedge	a piece of wood etc. which is thinner at one end than the other.	**whine**	1 a long, sad cry like the cry of a dog. 2 to complain a lot without good reason.
weed	1 a wild plant which grows where it is not wanted. 2 to dig out weeds.	**whip**	1 a piece of thin leather or cord on a handle, used for hitting things.
week	seven days.		2 to beat.

whirl	to spin round quickly.
whiskers	hair on the face (for example the long stiff hair at the side of a cat's mouth).
whisper	to speak very quietly.
whistle	1 a high, shrill note made by blowing through the lips and teeth. 2 an instrument for making a high note.
white	1 the colour of clean snow. 2 the part of an egg round the yolk.
whole	complete, with nothing missing.
wick	the string which burns in candles and oil-lamps.
wicked	very bad, evil.
wicket	1 the three stumps and their bails in cricket. 2 the cricket pitch.
wide	not narrow, broad.
widow	a woman whose husband is dead.
widower	a man whose wife is dead.
wife	a married woman.
wig	false hair to cover the head.
wigwam	a North-American Indian's tent.
wild	1 not tame, fierce. 2 not looked after by people. 3 out of control.
wilderness	a wild place where few plants grow and no one lives.
will	1 a written piece of paper saying who is to have a person's belongings when the person is dead. 2 the power to choose what you want to do.
willow	a kind of tree with thin drooping branches.
win	to be first or do best in a competition, race or fight.
wind (rhymes with 'pinned')	quickly-moving air.
wind (rhymes with 'mind')	to turn round and round.
windmill	a building with a machine which is worked by the wind which turns the blades or sails.
window	an opening in the wall of a building to let light in.
wine	a strong drink made from the juice of crushed fruit, usually grapes.
wing	1 one of the two parts of a bird or an insect, used for flying. 2 a part of an aeroplane which keeps it in the air.
wink	to shut and open one eye.
winter	the coldest season of the year, between autumn and spring.
wipe	to dry or clean with a cloth.
wire	thin, metal thread.

wisdom	being wise.
wise	showing good sense, clever, understanding a lot.
wish	1 to want very much, especially something you are unlikely to get. 2 what you wish for.
wit	cleverness, quickness of mind.
witch	a woman who is supposed to have magic powers.
wither	(especially of plants) to become smaller, drier and paler.
witness	a person who sees something happen.
wizard	a man who is supposed to have magic powers.
wobble	to move unsteadily from one side to the other.
wolf	a wild animal like a large dog.
woman	an adult female person.
wonder	1 to be surprised at. 2 to want to know.
wonderful	very good or pleasant, amazing.
wood	1 a lot of trees growing together. 2 the material which trees are made of.
wool	1 the short, curly hair on the backs of sheep and lambs. 2 thread made from this, used in weaving, knitting, etc.
woollen	made of wool.

word	1 letters together which mean something when spoken or read. 2 a solemn promise.
work	something you do, especially for payment.
world	the earth; all human beings together.
worm	a long, thin animal with a soft body that lives in soil.
worn	when something has been used so much that it is of little further use.
worry	to feel anxious or troubled.
worse	not as good as, less well.
worth	value.
wound	an injury where the skin is cut.
wrap	to put a covering closely round (something).
wreath	a ring of leaves or flowers specially made.
wreck	to smash up completely.
wren	a kind of very small, brown bird.
wrestle	to struggle with a person and try to throw him or her to the ground, sometimes as a sport.
wriggle	to twist the body about.
wring	to twist and squeeze (something) tightly to get water out.
wrinkle	a line or crease on the skin or in material.

wrist — the joint between the hand and the arm.

write — to put words or letters on paper (for example so that they can be read and understood).

wrong — not right, not correct.

X x

X-ray — a special photograph of the inside of your body, for example.

xylophone — a musical instrument played by hitting bars of wood or metal with a small hammer.

Y y

yacht — a light sailing boat, often used for racing.

yard —
1 a measure of length, equal to three feet.
2 a piece of ground next to a building with a fence or wall around it.

yawn — to open the mouth and breathe in and out deeply, especially when tired or bored.

year — a period of time equal to twelve months; the time that the earth takes to go once round the sun.

yeast — a substance used in baking bread to make the dough rise, and also in making beer or wine.

yell — to shout very loudly.

yellow — the colour of a lemon or the yolk of an egg.

yesterday — the day before today.

yet —
1 until now.
2 still.

yew — an evergreen tree with red berries.

yield —
1 to give way; to give in.
2 to produce (fruit or crops).

yogurt — a sour food made from milk, sometimes flavoured with fruit.

yolk — the yellow centre part of an egg.

young — not old.

youth —
1 the time when you are young.
2 a young man.

Z z

zebra — an African animal like a small horse with black and white stripes.

zero — the number 0, nothing.

zigzag — to move sharply to one side and then to the other.

zinc — a whitish metal.

zip — a sliding fastener used on clothes.

zone — a district, an area.

zoo — a place where wild animals are kept so that people can look at them.